Introduction to Knifemaking

by
SLSells

Published in the United States of America
All work Copyright 2014 retained by Steve Sells
Unless otherwise noted.

IBSN 978-1-312-68430-0 Paperback
IBSN 978-1-312-70984-3 Hardcover
Printed in the United States of America
First printing December 2014
Second Edition September 2015
Third Edition September 2018
Published by Fenris Forge, and Iforgeiron under license.

Table of Contents

6

Preface

I began my blacksmithing experience learning the basics of smithing under Fred Oden. One of the earliest surprises was that he was not going to have me make a real blade anytime soon. Before I could expect to make a good blade, I first had to learn fire control and how to move metal. I did not give up, even when Fred set my work station next to the belt grinder and only allowed me the use of a hand file to remove all my hammer marks. I kept at it, and soon learned not to leave marks. Thanks Fred, I

Illustration 1: Steve at the grinder.

owe you so much for that lesson-it has made the rest of my smithing career so much more productive, even if I was not to happy about it at the time.

Shortly after starting to understand the basics of the craft, I got married, relocated, and was able to start my blade apprenticeship under Bill Wyant of Avalon

Ironworks. I was excited that I found a bladesmith to train me, but soon learned Fred was easy-going in his shop compared to what I was in for now. Bill expected perfection in just about everything. But he also took the time to show me how to get to that level, and I soon learned he was not asking anything of me in the shop that he did not expect from himself. He said his clients deserve the best, and we have to deliver a few steps above what they expect.

After almost 6 years Bill's day job required that he move out of state, and I was left to work on my own. That is when I started up Fenris Forge. Bill gave me my first hammer, tongs and anvil, which I since have learned came to me from his teacher. Bill has passed on to his final rest since then, but I pray he knows I am passing on the many things he shared with me. I instruct my students to do the same when they are able. I am also fortunate to have had his instructor Dr. Jim Hrisoulas of Salamander Armory, take time to help continue my learning with tips and a few assignments to aid in stretching my abilities.

This book is dedicated to Fred and Bill, and the time they took showing me the path of Tubal-cane and the other masters of this craft. I also dedicate this book to the memory of my late father Lloyd Sells, who always encouraged my efforts to learn, and my wife Cherese for putting up with me all these years and letting me put a forge in our back yard.

Forward

The goal of this entire exercise has been simply to provide information that will be of value for anyone that wishes to read – or, better yet - will take that information to the shop and produce something. No matter what you make, I hope that this may help move you along in your work. It does not have to be a finely crafted and expensive blade, what matters is that I have assisted you in translating your vision of a blade into the real world.

For many of you, this will be as close to a one-on-one training session as you can get. I wish to help people learn to make the best blades they can. On the Internet forums I have seen photos of some good starts, but also have seen issues preventing those good starts from being as good as they could have been. I plan to address those issues and provide solutions!

This book will cover both high-tech and no-tech solutions to appeal to all abilities and resources.

To get the most from this tutorial, I suggest that you make sure you can move hot metal in a predictable manner. Make it wider, longer, tapered, and thinner. These are all of the things a blade needs to do, such as going from round to an elongated rectangle in a manner that to the best of our abilities, eliminates hammer marks.

This book will teach you more about fire management so you can end up with a blade without severe scaling or areas that have been burned and ruined.

I want you to learn the language of knife making. If you review all of the steps and terms used in heat treat process, you will be better able to follow what I mean when I use those terms in a next step. I have noticed a need and stepped up to see if I can help blade makers in a step-by-step way that will benefit a large number of smiths.

When a maker reaches a high level of skill, improving on that does not happen often. We search long and hard for ways to improve. Those improvements are often tiny but do add up. If I was just beginning and had this material presented to me, I would try and make what the lesson showed. I would spend some time in the shop and make a small pile of those items, trying to learn as much as possible. I would compare my work with the plan and make changes until I had the full benefit of the lesson, marking each and every item and looking for progress, before moving onto the next section. I recommend you do the same

What you do with this information is up to you. It is your shop, your work, and your schedule. I am attempting to share what I have learned during my growth as a smith. I hope I can assist you in your efforts to be the best blade smith you can.

Steve Sells

Acknowledgments

Shannon Davis-George, Editor. Without her efforts this would be just a very hard-to-read mess with a few photos.

Cherese Sells, My wife, who along with Shannon, proof read all this text, helping to make me look good.

Dan Stotland, Offering review and commentary, and sometimes offering additional text to clarify ideas I was attempting to share.

Glenn Conner, Publisher. Glenn has helped me get this information together in a form that is available to more people than I ever imagined.

Douglas Barlow, Photographer, Doug took the photos of me working in the forge. Photo numbers 1,2,3,10-21,30,35,36.

Rick Barrett, Bladesmith. Rick granted me the use of Photo number 25 of his Katana in the heat treating section on page 67.

Dominick Manco, Illustrator, Dominick provided the illustration on page 189.

iforgeiron.com My online host. The site started this entire process by providing the weekly online chat room where the ideas that were the beginnings of this book got started back in 2008. The premise was that a handful of blacksmiths could get together and talk about making sharp shiny things and, at the same time help others to improve their skills. Much of this book was inspired by the membership attending these chats, coming up with some wonderful questions and some strange ideas in a casual online environment.

Chapter 1

Getting Started

The tools needed in a general smithing shop apply to making blades as well. What we really need for a shop are the following:

- Proper protection and clothing
- First aid kit
- Fire extinguisher
- CO/CO2 monitor
- Heat source
- Hammer
- Tongs
- Anvil
- File

Lets talk about what we need to make a knife. It is easy to see the flashy things such as the new wonder steel, a new 18 inch grinder with 10 inch platen and 30 Hp reversible motor, etc. We have all seen this stuff advertised, but what is needed to make a knife?
First, lets ask the question "What is a knife?" It is a

tool we use to cut without cutting ourselves. If we can understand that, then everything else is extra.

Some get the wrong idea about a blacksmith shop, so let me be clear. Honestly we are the most dangerous thing in our shops. Any tools we have we must learn to use safely. We should demand everyone in our shops wear safety glasses. If you are wearing normal sun glasses, you need to stop before you go blind slowly.

The potential problem is called retina burn. I spoke with my eye Doctor and he suggested I get proper IR filters like rose-one. These are actual filters for reducing the Infra-Red (IR) light from a blacksmiths forge.

Having simple tinted glasses are not safe, because they do not target the IR wavelengths. So while they are reducing general ambient light levels, the glasses are causing your iris to open up and allow in more of the IR light. Doctors used to advise wearing Didymium filters, which were the only ones available 20 years ago, but they were designed for glass blowers, and not the IR for the temperates emitted by a forge. In most cases clear lenses are fine, but if you need some type of tinting, make sure they are the correct ones and speak with your eye Doctor.

Along with proper eye protection, I recommend wearing only natural fiber clothing at all times. Man made fibers melt and then stick like honey – over 2000 degree Fahrenheit honey. Whereas natural fibers only burn until we wet them down. This includes foot wear.

Equipment

An anvil can be a salvage yard scrap large enough to take the beating we are going to be doing on it. Buying a nice anvil can be expensive, but buying one used can get you the most bang for the buck. Expect to pay from $2 to $4 a pound for quality anvils in the 100 to 150 pound range on the used market. Forget trying to get one from an antique dealer; they demand top dollar. But if you let your friends and neighbors know you are looking for an anvil, sooner or later someone will tell you about one.

One word of warning is to beware of the painted lady. A painted anvil may look pretty but you should inspect it for cracks and weld lines, which are hard to see under a few coats of paint. These may still be perfectly serviceable but should result in a lower price for purchase if they have been repaired.

I suggest you acquire a good set of files and a file card for cleaning them. You will use these for many things in the shop. A bastard file with one flat side and one curved side is a good first file, along with a finer-tooth flat file with no teeth on its edges for the bevels and a few small chain saw sharpening files for detail work. As you use the files they will collect little bits from the work; a simple light tap on the work bench will usually dislodge these, though I occasionally will have to use a file card to clean the teeth. If you dust the file's teeth lightly with chalk when you begin using them, the chalk will fill the low spots of the file and make it cut smoother. This also allows for easier cleaning.

A hammer can be a chunk of metal light enough to swing comfortably with a smooth face but heavy enough to move hot metal. A hammer weighing 2 to 3 pounds is a suggested starting point. I do not suggest using a carpenters framing-type hammer; you will want a harder and larger face. You can buy a two pound sledge hammer from a local hardware store. As purchased it may not be usable for knife making. The hammer may have a rough face, and, in many cases edges that are too square which will leave marks in the work. You can fix this by smoothing one of the faces into a slight arch.

Your files should be able to remove steel, so we can do the needed changes by only using files.

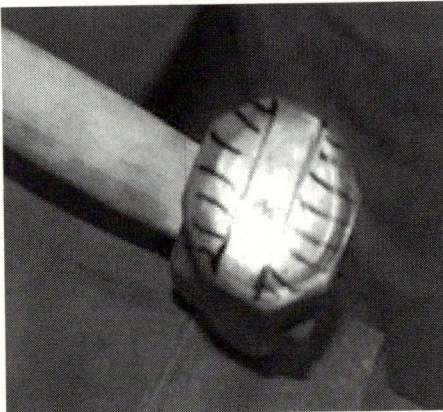

Illustration 2: Marked for removal.

Using a Sharpie® marker, I mark the hammer face where I need to remove steel. I prefer to do one hammer face like this, and leave the other one for drawing. It would have to have more radius on the edges but it does work.

In addition to a file, you could use an angle grinder for these modifications. Many can be found at the big box stores or pawn shops. They use replaceable 4 to 6 inch disks. Find one that is on sale with a couple of grinding wheels, a few cut off wheels, and a few flap wheels for finishing this hammer.

For the other hammer face I choose to do a cross peen for drawing out the metal faster. I marked the face for a guide and started grinding. As I grind it will heat up from the friction, so I dip in water now and then to keep it cool so it will not affect the heat treat of the hammer head or burn the handle that was left attached. I use a good belt grinder with good belts for these changes.

After removing the excess material, I round the peen in both directions, including rolling the corners on each end and making a blunt peen with no

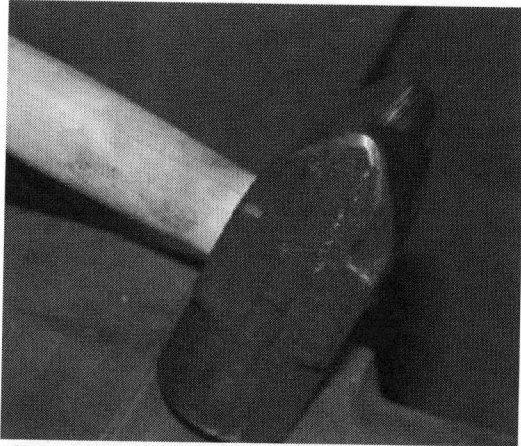

Illustration 3: Peen created after removal of metal.

corners. Corners leave dents you have to deal with in finishing a blade. Then I reshape the handle. I remove a bit of wood until the grip fells good in my hand. I do not want the handle perfectly round, a slight oblong shape makes it easy to know where the peen and face is located.

Grip the handle on your hands and see how it feels. If you shaped it correctly you can spin it around to switch between the face and peen by feel of the handle and not have to stop and look. Also, is should feel comfortable and not off balance in both positions.

Once you make these adjustments, test the hammer. You want it to move metal fast. The peen end does that. You want the flat end to make things right and flatten all of the dents you create with the peen end.

For example, to test the hammer modifications, I hammered onto a wooden 2x4 and found the the peen end was fine. The face, however had too much of a dome, leaving shallow bowl-like dents, so I went to the grinder. After flattening the face more with the grinder, I redressed the edges so they do not leave dents. If you hold a straight edge across the face you can see the contour easily. When testing again, I found the modifications seemed to be right.

Anvil height is paramount also. If, when you hammer, you find you are leaving dents on the far side, this can mean that your anvil is sitting too low. If hammer marks are on the near side it is too high. Adjusting your anvil to the correct working height will go a long way towards not leaving hammer marks, which in turn leaves you with a better finish to your work.

Next you need something to assist you in holding the hot steel. To start you can hold the cold end of longer sections of steel, but sooner or later you will need a set of tongs. Making your own tongs is the least expensive way, but there is nothing wrong with using a simple pair of pliers or vise grips for holding the stock until you can make your own pair of tongs.

Building your Fire

A fire pot can be as simple as a hole in the ground. Smiths have used this method for thousands of years; I prefer to stand while working.

An old grill can be converted to a forge with an old hair dryer for air (disable the heating element). A more solid unit can be built using a car brake drum and an air pipe welded to the bottom. Or you can purchase a ready-made forge from various manufactures.

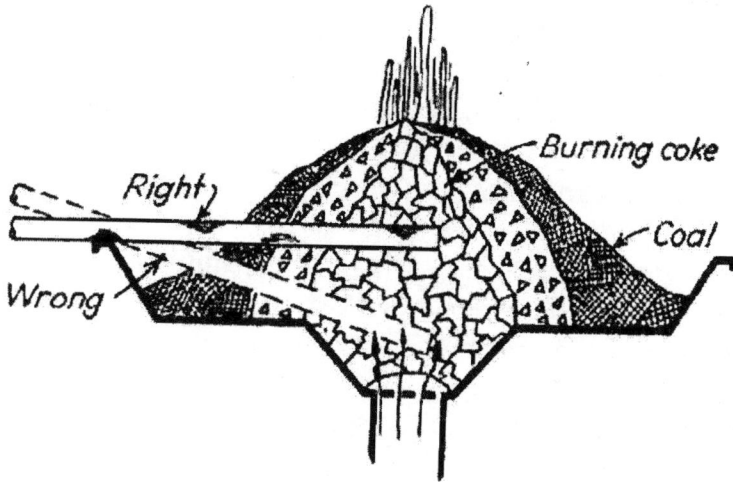

Illustration 4: Positioning of stock in a fire .

Charcoal was the standard fuel for centuries, and in more recent times coal has become a favorite for many smiths. Propane forges are something to consider as well. There are many plans on the Internet for building many types of forges. I suggest you start by looking at blacksmithing web sites, such as www.iforgeiron.com, which has been around for many years. They even provide many ideas and designs for how to build a forge yourself. Plus, its free to join.

Before you start to build your own forge, try to connect with a local blacksmithing group. Most places in the United States have a local group. Many meet monthly, while others meet more often. This way you can get hands-on experience before setting up a shop of your own.

Most groups provide forges, fuel, steel, and tools for use at these gatherings. They are great places to meet other people interested in this craft and experience different set-ups and the ways other people do things. You may also find good used tools for sale at a reasonable price from another member. Some members will even help you make your own tools.

A few hours working with an experienced smith will give you more information about running a forge and managing the fire than you can figure out from a book. It is hard to show proper air flow and fire maintenance in a book, or by doing it alone on your own. Most groups allow visitors, so bring safety glasses, and a cup of coffee to the meeting and have fun. Even if you choose not to join them, you will save yourself a lot of trouble, being able to use their equipment and being shown how to start and manage the forge before you start to design and build one of your own.

If you need further assistance getting set up or understanding the basics of smithing, I strongly suggest the book 'The Backyard Blacksmith" by Lorelei Sims, as well as the multi book series "The Skills of a Blacksmith" by Mark Aspery.

Design

A knife is an assembly of pieces. Hopefully each part will complement the others. I like to have a plan in my head or on paper before I make any blade.

Before we can do anything, you need to choose a blade type. There are some shapes that have been around for hundreds of years, because they work. The fantasy shapes from the many video games may look cool, but many do not function in the real world. In the past people needed blades for survival, so if a design did not work, the end user could have died as a result.

The purpose and planned use of the knife is the real starting point. You cannot decide what is the best design with out knowing what your blade must do. For example, a shaving razor will not use the same criteria as a fillet knife. Here are some things to consider when choosing your blade type:

- A shaving razor has no need to flex, and is normally taken well care of, so edge holding ability and being comfortable to hold are all that matters.
- If you want the knife to slice your food you will need some flex, a blade that is not too long and strength for when you cut into bone.
- Cleavers take abuse while performing heavy chopping. Like with an axe, edge holding is going to take a back seat to impact resistance.
- For a fillet knife, flexing is paramount.

Any time we combine multiple jobs into one blade, we have to compromise some functioning. For example, a hunting knife needs to do all of these, so they do none really well.

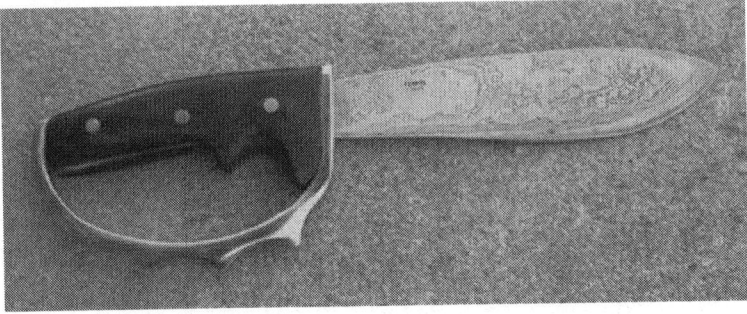

Illustration 5: Fighting blade.

The blade in this first photograph is a kukri inspired fighting knife with a D-guard.

You can refer to the blade in this picture as a dagger, which is common language for many types of double edged blades.

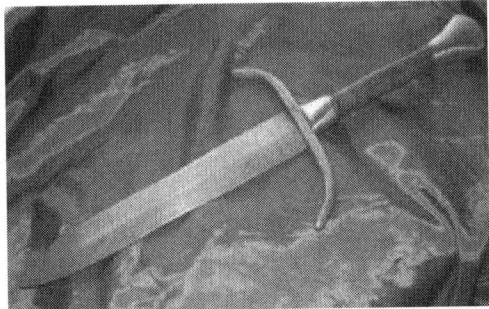

Illustration 6: Damascus dagger.

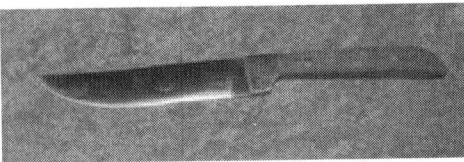

Illustration 7 Hunting knife with a tapered tang

This picture shows a fully tapered tang which is the rear portion of the blade that is inside the handle. The steel plates positioned between the blade and the tang are called bolsters. They are being held in position with pins through one side, through the blade, and out the other side. These pins are hammered down to become rivets and when ground flush, the pins do not show. Assembly of this is detailed in chapter seven.

This is a simple skinning knife. The tang only enters the handle about half way and is held in place with a pin.

Illustration 8: Skinning knife.

Another blade style is the Bowie. No one knows what the real Bowie knife looked like. There are some thoughts that the spine was straight all the way to the tip. However, if you look at places that sell Bowies, they most likely will have a cut or swoop in the top of the blade, as seen in this example.

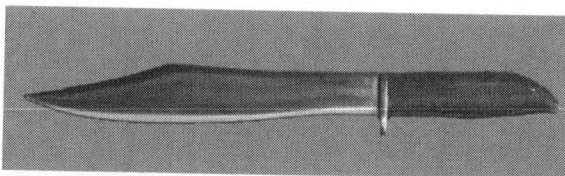

Illustration 9: Bowie.

There are no hard rules on what you call a knife. However if you use common shape names most people will know what you are talking about.

Chapter 2

Choosing Steel for Blades

Choosing the correct steel is the first step in making any blade. Getting steel is a lot like buying beef. A dead cow laying in the sun for a day or two is still beef, but it is not quite food quality meat. Found and reclaimed steel is in many ways the same. There is no way to tell about abuse from its past usage. Any fractures in the steel can be a problem later, and not knowing what alloy it is makes heat treating problematic as well.

There are exceptions to everything I state here. Metallurgy is a complex field, but I am presenting this information in an easy to understand way, so you can use this information to decide what steels to use for making your blades.

Most steel manufacturing specifications will not have an exact amount of an added element, instead a range will be declared. This is because of many factors that can happen in the manufacturing process. All steels contain a low level of impurity elements that result from the steel making process. These impurities can be eliminated from laboratory-prepared steels where cost is not a problem. However industrial steel is produced in mega-tonnage quantities, and economic production processes result in low levels of certain impurity elements present in steel.

What is Steel

Steel at its simplest is a mix of iron (**Fe**) and carbon (**C**). When carbon is present in amounts of over 2.5% the mix is referred to as Cast Iron. In most cases getting even close to this high of carbon content is not good in a blade steel. Most blade steels are in the range of .50% to 1.20% carbon.

Steels containing the higher amount of carbon in this range are very good for smaller blades. Steels with a carbon content in the lower range are often used for larger blades, and even swords. This is not a hard and fast rule as there are makers such as Howard Clark, that do use a higher carbon steel, such as SAE number 1086, in making swords.

Its your shop, so your rules apply. Consider for a moment how many people have received a paper cut, but no one would want to buy a knife made from paper. Some people use Rail Road spikes, even though the ones labeled HC are only 0.30% carbon at best and will never give a great edge by themselves. Titanium will not harden or hold an edge well, but it can be useful as a scuba diving knife. Take some time to think about what is in your steel before you begin.

I strongly suggest you start with one grade of steel and stay with that for a while, learning all you can before attempting a new steel. If you jump around trying out various steels, you will learn less because each steel moves differently, and you will need to make some adjustments to work it properly.

Additional Elements in Steels

Today manganese (**Mn**) is present in most all commercial steels as a deoxidizer and can help overcome problems with the sulfur embrittlement that causes hot shortness. This is a condition where the metal crumbles when forged at high temperatures. This element is not the same as magnesium (**Mg**). Some people confuse these, so I thought it best to state it plainly here. Manganese aids in the hardening process, and would be added in the amounts of 0.30% to 0.75% in most of the steels we can access for use. The lower levels of this addition are better for the formation of a Hamon (the cloud-like pattern near the cutting edge on a differentially heat treated blade), but higher additions make a steel stronger.

Another common addition to steel is a carbide former known as chromium (**Cr**). Added in small amounts helps steel be deep hardening. Normally about 0.8% to 1.5% chrome is added. Steel grade 5160 is a very common choice from this group. This steel is basically like a simple 1060 with the addition of 0.8% chrome, and ANSI type D-2 has about 12% total. At higher levels of chrome other things can happen, and when there is more than 10.5% free chrome in the mix, it is referred to as a stainless steel.

Molybdenum (**Mo**) aka moly is another carbide forming addition usually added small in amounts of around 0.1% to 0.4%. A little of this element goes a long way in steel. Higher additions make steel hard to work even when glowing at a bright yellow heat. M-2 is a good example of a steel with high amounts of moly.

Nickel (**Ni**) is not a carbide former but is added often to assist other elements such as chrome, in grain refinement, toughness, and strength. It is used in high amounts in some stainless steels. Amounts of about 2% may be in low alloy steels such as L-6 or 15N20, and up to 35% or so for some stainless steels. A nickel-bearing steel is a common choice for the bright layers in a pattern welded blade.

Silicon (**Si**) is also added to blade steels in amounts from 0.3% to 2.5% to aid in toughness and strength . When silicon is added in higher amounts it increases the conductivity and is used in the electrical field. Steel grade 9260 is a good steel for large blades with about 2% silicon.

Tungsten (**W**) and/or Vanadium (**V**) can also be added to retard grain growth of the steels. These metals assist in keeping grains smaller in a finished blade and raise the tempering temperature. Usually added in the amount of 0.1% to 0.35%, higher additions of these elements cause the steel to be very hard to move under the hammer. Many of the properties of these two elements that are of interest to the bladesmith are very similar when used in knife steels, so I address them together here.

To be clear, we do not add these elements to our existing steel inventory. Steels are purchased with these additions already in the alloy. This is only a start and is not a complete listing. This is just an overview to assist in sorting out the variety of some common steel alloy elements and what they can do for us as blade makers. I hope this explanation helps you understand what some of the steel additions have to offer for your blades.

SAE Steel Codes

Plain carbon	10XX
Manganese	13XX
Nickel alloy	2XXX
Nickel/Chrome	3XXX
Molybdenum	4XXX
Chromium steel	5XXX
Chrome/vanadium	6XXX
Nickel/Chrome/Moly	8XXX
Manganese/Silicon	9XXX

See the Appendix at the end of this book for a more comprehensive listing, which includes an alloy analysis of specific steels I have used.

The "X" in the last 2 or 3 places designates the amount of carbon. For example 5160 would have close to 0.6 percent of carbon, also referred to as 60 points of carbon. Normally the actual amount is within a range of the stated amount.

Another example would be the carbon content of 1086, which should be around 0.86%, though it will actually be between approximately 0.83% and

0.90%. This explains why two different batches of the same grade of steel can work and harden differently. Steel types 1084 through 1095 are very common blade choices from this group.

AISI Steel Codes

A   Air hardening alloys
D   Die steel alloys
F   Tungsten alloys
H   Hot work alloys
L   Low alloy
M   Molybdenum alloys
O   Oil hardening alloys
P   Mold steel alloys
S   Shock resistant steels
W   Water hardening steels

There will be numbers to designate the various differences in alloy. W-series and F-series steels make very good blades. The F-series is no longer being commercially produced, but W-2 is common enough and can give a nice Hamon.

To be able to identify the various steels I label each end of every bar of all my orders as they come in. The mills may have color codes painted on the ends for them to keep things sorted. Each mill may use a different steel ID color coding than another mill. For example, just because a bar may have blue paint on one end, does not guarantee it is 1084.

Contrary to what a few may try to lead you to believe, there is no way to tell the different alloys apart by feel. If you choose not to label the order when received, you may regret it in the future when you find that long forgotten bar of steel.

Making your First Blade

Before making quality blades we need to learn how to move steel in a manner we can control. I am not going to show you how to build a forge. There are many great books that already cover that, and I am assuming you have already learned some basic forge skills.

Knife making is not a good place to start as a first project. Since I know it's too much to ask you to read this entire book before trying to make a blade, let's just jump in and attempt a blade anyway. Do not expect a perfect blade your first time. You can still learn a lot from jumping in and getting it out of your system.

I used less than a one gallon bucket of coal for this blade. The steel for this blade I used was an old coil spring from a junk yard. I needed to test this steel to see if it would be usable for making blades. After I got the coil back to my shop, I heated the steel to a point where a magnet would not stick and allowed it to air cool, to see if this coil would air harden and it did not, because a file would still cut it. If this steel was hard enough to skate a file after air cooling from its non-magnetic point, I would have to anneal it to be able to work with files and abrasives after forging and before hardening and tempering. See chapter four, for more detailed information on making the steel as soft as it can be to make that work a little easier.

Then I heated the steel again to that same point, and

quenched in oil preheated to 120F. A file would not cut it at all after cleaning the scale off, so I knew it would harden when I was ready for the hardening part. If it had not hardened in oil I would have heated it again and used a brine solution to quench. A brine is made by dissolving as much salt as possible into warm water. If that did not work then I would know I could not use this metal for a blade.

Using found steel or unknown for this first blade had some potential drawbacks, including the following:

- The carbon content may have been too low to be hardenable for blades.
- The steel could already have cracks too small to see without a microscope.
- The cost involved in acquiring this steel, including the drive time and fuel costs, could have exceeded the cost of purchasing new steel.
- There was a risk of this having been contaminated steel.

It just may be better to have a known steel shipped to your shop or home. To decide if a found steel is usable, using proper protection, forge the steel down to blade thickness. Once reaching a thickness of about 1/4 inch, heat to the point where a magnet will no longer be attracted to it, and allow the steel to cool in still air.

Cut this piece into two sections. Take one section and heat to where a magnet will no longer attract, then quench it in oil heated to about 120F. Remember the color of the steel when it was at the point where the magnet would no longer stick to it.

Caution: The oil may flare up. Using gloves and a pair of tongs will protect your hands. Keep the container mostly full to reduce the air pockets that feed a fire, but not too full, to prevent you from slopping burning oil on shop floor. Finally, hold the tang at an angle rather than in line with the blade to keep away from the flames. When you see the swirling of the oils, slow or stop and wait 30 seconds more. Then you can remove the steel from the quench. A hinged lid on the container can be flipped into place and suffocate any flames though they usually go out fairly quickly on their own. Using proper protective gear, gloves, face shield, and proper clothing, break the steel section in half. Examine the break; you should see that the grain should be nice and fine-sized, which is just what you want for a blade.

Take the other section you cut off and heat to above forging temperatures to the point when it starts to sparkle, and then quench that in the same oil. Break this in half the same way you did the first piece. Notice the difference in the force needed to break it? Take a look at the grain of the steel at this break. This second piece was only to show you an example of large grain, which we do not want. Remember this, because if you let your steel get too hot, this is the effect it will have on your blades internal structure and strength.

Now we know the rest of this coil spring is a type of steel suitable for making a blade we can trust. We have found a

Illustration 10: Starting to flatten the bar.

heat treat method that works for this spring. Other springs or found steel may be different, so they also need to be tested. This method will help you see if what you have is usable.

For now all that matters is that your steel can be hardened. In chapter four I will explain the details about what happens in the hardening process. Now lets get a blade into shape.

Getting the Steel Flat

To move steel from rounds to flat I prefer using the peen like in this example.

Illustration 11: Widening the bar.

I start making a round stock piece into a blade from the tip end, leaving excess steel for me to hold. After getting it wider with my diagonal peen, I flatten it a bit more with the face of the hammer as I move down the blade towards the ricasso.

You want this blade to be flatter and wider. You could choose to work the other way around, starting with the tang and work forward. It is entirely up to you. Take it to 1/3 of your desired thickness to avoid making the steel too thin compared to the parent stock. Thin sections will over heat when you try to get the thick sections near them heated.

You can cut the end into a 45 degree angled point with a chisel, but I prefer to forge the point. That may work for some, while others may use an angle grinder or hot cut. Just make sure the point you forge angles down, meaning that the longer part of the point will be the

Illustration 12: Flattened and tip formed.

cutting edge. As you form the edge it curves back up when you forge the bevels, to become the knifes spine.

Flatten the blade out with the modified face of the hammer. One thing to remember when fullering a blade for width is not to go too far. If you go too deep, you will have hammer marks that are difficult to remove.

Illustration 13: See the other blade I used as a pattern?

Using the flat face of the hammer, take the sharp edges off of the steel, but do not worry about the saw marks where you cut it. A small radius fuller leaves marks you do not want to try and remove with a file. One of the biggest mistakes I see is hammer marks on the ricasso. If you do not put the hammer marks there, you will not have a problem.

Notice the metal pattern being used as a guide for this blade in photo 13. Contact with the scale or a hot blade will not light it on fire. The pattern was lying to my left on my work table. Some choose to leave it on the stump.

When I flatten the blade with flat faces on both sides, tongs that are positioned to hold on the ricasso will protect that area. The tong jaws also may rest at the edge of your anvil and if you put them in the same place every time when you do bevels, both sides will have ricasso bevel junction at the same place.

Let's take a moment to discuss materials and quality of work. Keep in mind that it is your shop, and you make the rules and can change them whenever you wish. If you make cheap knives, you will sell cheap knives. Excellence is a decision. Talent is not necessary for excellence, but persistence is. If you wish to make nice knives, decide at some point what is the worst knife you will allow to leave your shop. Once you do that, look at each piece before it leaves to see if it meets your expectations.

Mystery steel is just that. You can do many things to it, like the hardening testing methods I covered earlier in this chapter. That will not tell you the steel type, but I knew it was a piece of a coil spring because I had purchased it myself, and found I could harden it. Those tests told me I we could make a blade from it.

I advise to not use spark testing because it is not reliable, nor is it a method you can learn quickly. By the time you learn to do it well, you may have already found out what I will cover next.

Let's think about mystery steel some more. What does it cost to go find steel that may in fact not work for a blade? How far will you drive and what does driving cost for that two way trip? I gave that up years back. I can phone a number, and in less than a couple of days have steel sent to me and know exactly what type of steel it is, as well as exactly what it takes to heat treat it. I can select the right steel for what I intend to make with it. I pay about $14 for a 4 ft long bar of 1084 measuring 1/8 inch thick x 1 1/4 inch wide.

People have been talking about rail road spike knives and other non-blade material to fashion blade-like objects. Remember at best it's 0.30% carbon; and that is not enough to get very hard. The High Carbon designation in that case is relative only to other spikes. It is only a large nail.

Even your super-duper magic quench cannot change physics. You cannot get a good edge from rail road spikes alone. We can sharpen them to have a cutting edge, but it will not hold the edge long. But we can cheat. We are smiths, so we forge weld a high carbon steel bit to where we want our cutting edge to be, and we solve that problem. If you insist on using spikes, at least take the steps needed to make them into a quality blade. They will look the same, but using a steel such as 1080 or even a higher carbon content section for the cutting part, will hold that edge a long time. I will go into more detail about forge welding in Chapter nine.

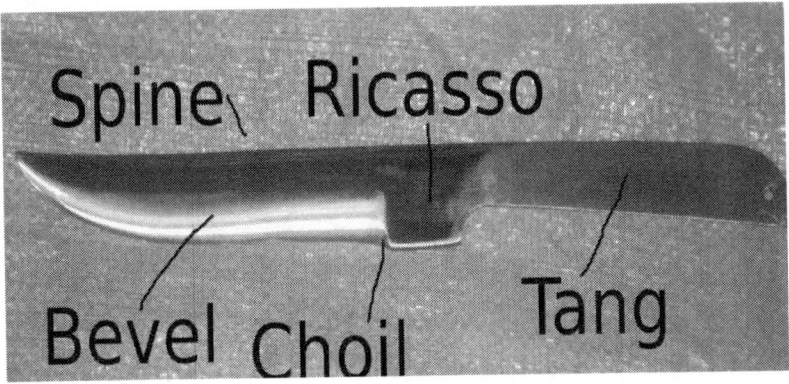

Chapter 3

Forging

Bevels

Chapter two covered the drawing out of your steel into a blade like form. Now we proceed to forming the bevels, which are the angled sides of the blade that allow the mass of the blade to flow into the cutting edge.

The ricasso should be forged flat and a bit thicker than it will be in a finished blade. If you protect that area with the tongs like in figure 14 you will not make

Illustration 14: Starting the bevel.

hammer marks in it. The blade is still thick at this point. Flip the blade over often and hammer from the other side; the anvil does not leave hammer marks. You do not have to practice this technique on a blade.

To make a bevel, lift the spine a little bit and change the angle at which you strike to hit more towards the edge, then flip the blade and repeat on the other side. Pick a steel you know will harden and make sure it has good grain size when you broke it in the test. Forged it to a pattern, watching out for hammer marks. Make sure that forging of the steel moves the metal where you wish it to be. You should have something like the pattern. Remember to flip the sides every 4 or 5 blows to keep the stress in the metal even. This can help prevent warping later in the process.

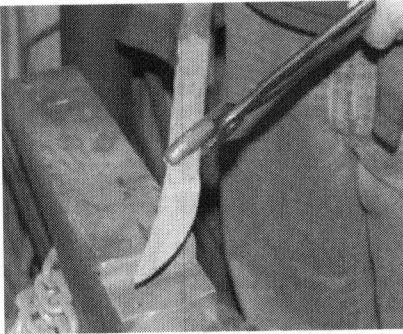

Illustration 15: Curving blade.

One question I get from beginners is how to prevent the blade from curving while they are hammering the bevels. The curving is simply a result of the metal being stretched on the one side of the blade and not the other.

All we need to do is to flip the blade 90 degrees so the warp is up and hit it a few times on the edge with the hammer to straighten it out again. Just take a couple of seconds and straighten blade out before it goes back in the fire. Make sure to lay the blade in the heat so that, when you pick it up, the side you wish to hit is face up on the anvil.

I am constantly straightening the spine as I forge the blade. Some choose to try pre-bending the spine in the wrong direction (reverse curving) before forging the bevels so the blade ends up being straight when finished. I feel that only works when you know ahead of time how much it will bend.

Illustration 16: Correcting a curve.

I simply adjust back to straight as I go, never letting it get too much curve in the first place. Because the metal is stretching as you forge the bevels, it hooks or bends. Correct that bend as you work. Do what feels comfortable to you. Some like to keep the spine facing towards them, others like it facing to the side, whichever is easier to hammer. If you are ambidextrous it may help to switch hands to get a better angle of attack.

Illustration 17: Finishing the bevels.

Do not let the blade lose color before reheating it. Keep color in mind as you work in different ambient light. The brightness you may see at dusk may not be the same in daylight or under shop lights. The biggest difference between general smithing and blade work is that we are now working with much higher carbon steels.

Whereas mild steel can be worked from near yellow heat down to a black heat, higher carbon steels have much narrower ranges for forging. If we work the metal too hot it can turn into cottage cheese. If we work it too cold it can spider web, and in both cases the blade may have to be scrapped.

When we move steel, it changes shapes in several ways. Learn how the metal feels when you hit it to judge forging temps. Once you have the blade near the length you want, go to a hot cut and remove some of the extra stock.

As I thin out this blade more near the tip it widens. Now it is more like I want and I will move the heat to the tang end to bring that end to the same width as the middle of the blade. As mentioned earlier, use tongs as a protection to keep from hitting the ricasso. Also make sure the tongs do not hit the side of the anvil.

When you flip the blade to work the other side, put the tongs back in same place and the start of the plunge cut will be almost perfectly in line side to side. Think again about hammer and anvil being top and bottom dies. If you lay the blade flat on the anvil and top strike to make a bevel, the bevel will be one sided. If you flip and repeat on the edge, the bevel will move over and lay flat on other side to match the anvil face.

It is too easy to leave marks you cannot remove, so use lighter blows and a lighter hammer as you near the end of forging. Take your time; do not rush.

I have a pattern next to the anvil most of the time and keep that in mind as I work. When I cut the end off, I laid the blade on the pattern to see if it matches.

Illustration 18: Planishing with the flat faced 2# hammer.

Sharpening

It may seem I am getting ahead of myself by talking about sharpening now. But you will need to know what is going to happen later, so you can get the bevels correct now. Of course, this is all dependent on the type of steel and how it is heat treated. Think about a couple of uses for blades. One could be a machete, while the other is a box cutter blade. A machete needs to flex so it can hack and chop. A box cutter slices; if you flex a box cutter, it will break. You could get both of those from similar types of blade steel, but the heat treat would differ a lot. The same is true with a straight razor. The blade is really hard, and it keeps a nice edge but will break if flexed.

The angle of this file to the blade will give a course edge. Think machete. Now you can change the angle so it will do a fine or keen edge. And you can use a more coarse angle or

Illustration 19: Filing at the choil.

a finer angle depending on the steel, the heat treat and the intended use.

This is a cross section of a box cutter blade. See the difference in the final edge? The first hollow ground right down to the edge would have to be completely reground to sharpen it. The box cutter just could be touched up on the angled edges and not move back onto the sides of the blade much at all.

This is a single bevel like I would use for a sushi knife.

Here is a blade cross section that has been hollow ground so the edges form the cutting edge.

This is a convex grind. Some call it an apple seed or channel grind. This works well for an axe or hatchet edge.

This is a flat ground blade with a more coarse angle for the edge. Think kitchen knives. I have heard other smiths say they flat grind a blade so that the edges meet and form the cutting edge like the box cutter. So if the flat ground edge gets dull, then just like the hollow grind I spoke of earlier, the blade has to be ground from the spine to the edge to renew the cutting edge. But if I put a second angle along the cutting edge like shown in this illustration the blade is easy to resharpen.

That final edge, whether on a flat ground or hollow ground, will only be needed to get the angle you want. That angle is based on the thickness of the blade.

You use knives almost daily. You dull them, then resharpen them. When you grind the edge down to where it meets the other side, the back side of the edge will develop what is called a wire edge. That is your cue to use a finer abrasive of your choice. Sharpening with a buffing wheel does not work. If you did that edge with a 120 grit go finer, you may need to use 220 grit. That will leave a smaller wire edge.

To feel the wire edge put your finger on the back side near the spine and push it lightly towards the edge. You will feel or may see a rough spot on the edge, and you can likely use a thumb to wipe it off. For a finer edge, finer abrasives are needed. A machete may be sharpened using a file, while a kitchen knife needs abrasives or stones.

Find the angle the blade had at the beginning. Duplicate that angle, as stated above, by starting back from the edge and rolling over to catch the edge, making a kind of a rocking motion. There are lots of little "tricks" like slack belt grinding and sharpening to get down to a wire edge. If you have a mystery metal and you do not want to gamble with it, use a file to check if it skates as a way of checking both the metal and the final outcome of the heat treat. Skate a file across the edge to see if it grabs or slides. Sliding is a sign of good hardening.

I buy my steel new and check with a file after hardening. It is a trusted method based on using a lot of those steels. I test each blade before I sharpen it.

The anvils smooth face gave my example blade a flat, even surface to work on; good hammer control keeps the blade surface smooth. I tested the steel and found it did not accidentally air harden so no need to anneal this blade. Now I am ready to work with the files.

Profiling

I used 2 files for smoothing the sides and bevels. One file is a medium-coarse tooth bastard file the other a fine tooth double cut file.

I use my vise to hold the blade for the file work. Then I can file the blade with it held in place. I do the ricasso area first and run the file onto the tang and then down the blade.

It is important to check the blade often to see that the sides are parallel and that you are not tapering it.

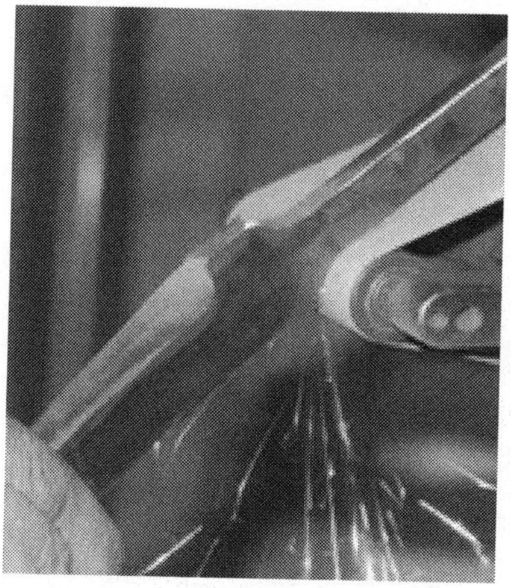

Illustration 20: Small wheel in use.

Eyeball for the parallel side. File at different angles to see high spots. And on this blade file lengthwise and in line with the blade to see peaks and valleys.

One more important item is the place where the ends of the ricasso meet the tang. If you leave a sharp corner that may create a place for a crack to develop in heat treat or in use.

Photo 20 shows my small wheel attachment used to radius the transition. If I were using a style where I needed a tighter bend, I would use a round needle file and make an arc at this transition.

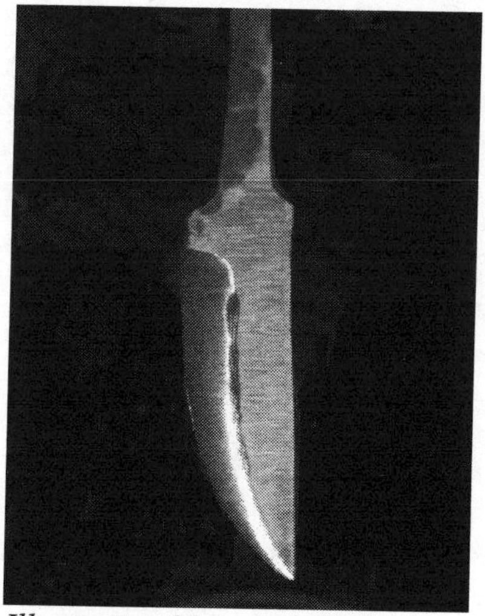

Photo 21 shows a blade with some scale spots that show rough file work. Those spots must come out. If you just file only those spots, there will be a big dip in that area of the blade. Be sure to file the whole length of the blade to remove these or you will have ripples in the finish.

Illustration 21: rough filed showing scale

Rough Grinding

I started with showing how to forge a blade using a bare minimum of tools. I will make more knives using tools that most consider the preferred tools for the task, as well as show you how I use them.

After I finish forging blades, most of those blades will need a polished finish on them. Hand filing and block sanding does work, and I will always use these tools, but to speed things up a bit, most blades end up getting finished on a powered grinding machine. I have a professional Bader B3© machine that has a 1.5 HP motor and it uses standard 2 x 72 inch belts. This is the most common belt size for knife makers, and has a very wide selection of belts available. I start with a Blaze brand belt in 40 grit; they are not cheap to buy, but for dollar vs. work, they are very cost effective.

This is the blade getting a few passes on the 40 grit. Start with the flats of the blade and get them parallel, removing all of the hammer marks that you can. Then clean the outer profile before proceeding to the cutting edge bevel.

Illustration 22: At the grinder with 40 grit.

At this point you have sharp edges and clean lines. If you are not used to using your eye to judge, layout fluid is great for marking off where you want to go. I choose to use a Permanent Marker. It does not wash off when cooling the blade in water. Mark where that bevel you are working on needs to go and grind up to that point. On larger blades, take it in smaller sections of 3 to 4 inches wide, and, after getting the entire blade length done, blend them in.

Another way to keep the flats FLAT rather than having waves, is to change the angle a bit and grind from end to end. This is also why I leave the tangs of my blades so long. It creates a hand hold, keeping fingers away from the belt. A ceramic belt at 5500 fpm will take off a finger's flesh to the bone before you notice. For safety I have a metal bucket below the grinder to catch the flash, sparks and hot metal dust. I can easily take off 3/16 inch from a blade in one pass with the 40 grit belt on this machine, though I normally do not need to remove that much.

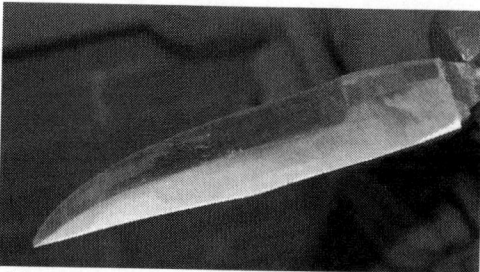

Illustration 23: After 220 grit.

After getting the 40 grit work completed, I move to a Norton© 120 grit and repeat this process. Changing the angle of the blade against the belt helps to see if the grind lines are removed from the prior grinding work. If the last grit was cutting across the blade, then the next should be at least at 45 degrees to the last grit marks.

Remember to finish removing all grind marks and scratches from the last grits passes before moving to the next finer grit. After I finish with the 120 grit, I move to the 220 grit. The blade is not hard at this point, meaning overheating in most cases will not harm the blade. To prevent pain in your fingers, keep a bucket of clean water close and dip the blade into it often to keep the blade cool. Be aware that some belts do not tolerate water, so I have a shop rag handy to dry the blade off after each dip.

The grinding process will make a mess of the area, spreading metal dust all over. A small trick to keep the belts clean, is to make a belt storage area between the studs in the walls of the shop. Keep the belts organized so you can find them fast for grit changes while grinding. I have wooden pegs to hang my belts from, but one could use nails to hang the belts, as well.

Illustration 24: Belt storage.

After your grinding progresses from 40 grit to 120 grit to 220 grit, the blade is ready for heat treating. (which will be explained in chapter four). There is no need to use any of the finer grits at this point. Some people only go as far as 120 grit before heat treating, but I feel this leaves marks that are deep enough to cause possible problems during the quench.

Remember after heat treating, you must be careful to keep the blade from getting hot, or you will ruin the temper, and will have to anneal and repeat the entire hardening and tempering process all over again.

Some people ask about whether to grind edge up or edge down. It all depends on what bevel is being worked. The simple answer is the side you are working on is up so you can look directly down on it to assure the proper angle at the grinder. I set the blades angles by eye, but I judge angles by eye often in my day job as an Electrician and constantly recheck with gauges to confirm, so I continually adjust my perception that way, as well. Use a gauge if you wish. There is nothing wrong with using tools to help you. I do not have the knife rest attached to the grinder. I tried to use it when I first began, and my teacher Bill Wyant took it off, demanding I train my eye. That has paid off well in the long run.

Chapter 4

Heat Treating Simple Steels

In this chapter I will cover what makes a blade-shaped object a functional knife. The information presented here is specifically tailored for blades. Thicker items will need different procedures than the thin cross sections we are dealing with in blades. Mill specs that come with an order of new steel are fine for dealing with cross sections that are inches of thickness, but these specs leave you, the poor blade smith, in the dark as to where to begin. For example, SAE steel type 1095 is fine with a water quench for a large tool, but if we use water for quenching a high carbon knife, the steel can crack from cooling too fast because of the thinness of the blade.

Steel is a metal that can take five basic crystal structural forms, also called phases:

- Cementite
- Ferrite
- Austenite

- Pearlite
- Martensite

With the proper manipulation of heat, we can change our steel from one form to another to affect the way the steel performs for us.

Determining Temperatures

You can purchase a thermometer to measure the inside of a forge, as well as the blade surface. This is the best way to determine the correct temperature of your steel. There is another way to control and identify the temperatures of your forge. For centuries smiths have used the colors put out from the fires and the steels surface to judge how hot it is. We all see color differently. In addition, changes in lighting will also effect the way we perceive colors. Here is a list to get you started.

°C	color	°F
199	straw	390
229	light straw	445
241	dark straw	465
250	brown	480
260	brown/purple	500
271	purple	520
282	dark purple	540
302	blue	575
427	dark gray	800
538	very slightly red	1000
590	slight red	1100
649	dull red	1200
705	medium red	1300

760	red	1400
815	bright red	1500
871	orange red	1600
930	orange	1700
982	orange yellow	1800
1040	dark yellow	1900
1093	bright yellow	2000

Within a short while, you too will be using color to accurately judge the heat of your forge, most smiths have learned to be accurate to between 25°F and 50°F. See color chart on reverse cover.

Below the 1000°F mark is what many smiths refer to as 'black heat'. This means that below this temperature the steel itself no longer puts out its own light, but the colors we are seeing are from the oxidation surface that reflects ambient light. More on this later.

Annealing

Sometimes steels can harden on their own. Before we can sand, grind, or file our work, we should get it into a soft state. There are various internal physical forms that steel can take, and various ways we can get the steels internal structures into those forms. Let's start by covering various methods of annealing, from simple to complex - to address the needs of steel workers.

First, try the simple method of bringing your steel to the austenitizing temperature and allowing to cool slowly. The austenitizing temperature is the temperature that the steel structure transforms to austenite. As you heat the steel, if you pay close attention, you can see the metal getting brighter and yellower as the temperature rises, and eventually you will notice the color quickly gets a little darker, then resumes its raise in color at this transition point.

Lucky for us there is an easy way to identify this point using a magnet, as steels are non-magnetic at the curie point. The color change I mentioned is very subtle, so trust the magnet. Allow a few more seconds of heating to let the metal get about 100° F warmer, and then you are at the austenizing temperature.

From here you will be allowing (even encouraging) the steel to cool as slowly as possible. This is usually done by placing the item in a 'hot box', which is a container that holds a loose insulating medium to retain the heat in the metal you place inside.

I like to use vermiculite, available from most garden centers; others have used, with good success, ashes or some other things to hold in the heat and slow down the rate of cooling. Some smiths will just allow the steel to remain in the gas forge after turning it off to cool down, with the residual heat in the forge slowing the cooling rate. What matters is to keep the steel hot for as long as possible. Many times this is all you need to do to get your steel soft enough to finish shaping.

Sometimes placing the blade into a hot box does not work, because the steel cools fast enough to at least partially harden on its own. This is most always the case with air hardening steels which require other methods to soften the steel. Most higher alloy steels can air harden to a point. I have had L-6 and even its cousin 15N20 air harden more than once in a hot box.

A method that works well, referred to as a sub-critical anneal, is where we take the steel up to the austenitizing temperature as normal, but, after air cooling, reheat to a temperature about 100°F to 200°F below the curie point, before allowing the steel to cool again in the hot box. What you have done here is to temper the steel at so high a temperature that it is at a very low hardness. In many cases this is enough to be able to work our steel.

Sometimes we have a steel (such as with a stainless steel) that will not get soft enough to grind well even with a ceramic 40 grit belt, so we try "spheroidal annealing". This process is best done with a temperature-controlled forge. After heating to the just above the austenitizing temperature, we use the forge to slowly cool the steel, at a controlled rate.

There are different cooling rate requirements for various types of steel. In most cases, maintaining a cooling rate of 40° - 50°F per hour until the steel temperature gets below 900°F is enough. Some steels may need as slow as 20 degree per hour drop rates.

What happens to the steel in this process is the carbon will collect into spherical ball shapes. Annealing only has the carbon returning to free flowing position in the steel lattice or collecting in the face of the steel cube-shaped matrix.

The steels grains grow quite large as well. This causes the steel to be in its softest state possible. Some blade steels come from the mill in this state, but many do not. I admit this is not easy, nor always possible in a coal forge. Even with a gas forge or electric oven it is costly to run for the required 14 hours or more.

I hope these three methods of softening steels I have shown will answer a few questions we all have had through our experience with working metal.

Hardening

In order for our newly made blade to hold an edge, we must get it hardened. Many have asked how to heat treat a blade. The following is a very basic primer on that process.

When we finish forging our blade, we have a knife-shaped object. We use thermal treatments to change the molecular arraignment of the crystals in the matrix to make it hard enough to hold an edge and actually be a blade. The following processes only work on steels with a carbon content of 30 points (0.30) or higher. If lower amounts of carbon are present the steel will not harden enough to make any real difference. For blades I prefer to have at least a level of .50 carbon.

At room temperature the structure of the steel is normally in a body-centered cubic structure. The cubes of steel have an iron atom at each of the 8 corners of the cube and carbon in the center of the box. This is called ferrite, which is very malleable. Ferrite can hold only a minimal amount of carbon, and it is relatively soft. But pearlite, or a combination of ferrite and cementite, has grain structures that resemble human fingerprints. Depending on who you ask, Steel with 0.77 or 0.84 percent carbon consists of uniform

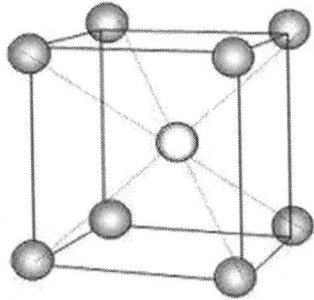

pearlite at room temperature and is known as being
eutectoid steel. I am one of the people that feels 0.84
is correct.

By heating the steel we can change the arrangement of
the carbon and iron, into a
face-centered cubic called
austenite, where iron is at the
8 corners, and carbon is on
the six sides of the cube. The
temperature at which this
occurs is called the
austenitizing temperature that
happens to be close to and
slightly above the curie temperature.

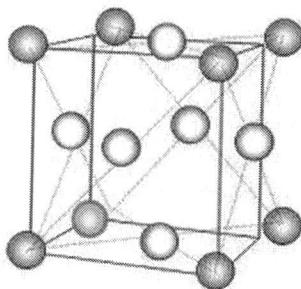

Normalizing is when we remove the steel from the
heat, and slowly allow it to air cool. Normalizing
allows stress of the metal to relax in the blade. Many
normalize three times to cycle the steel for grain
refinement as well as to insure there will be no
warping.

I like to drill a hole in the end of the tang for hanging
the blade from a wire to cool, after and sometimes
during the hardening process. The hole does not have
to be large, I use 1/8-inch drill bit and in most cases
this hole is never seen after the handle is in place. To
reduce scaling, some use a product called *Turco(tm)*
available from knife supply houses available in a
quart-sized can. Dip the ready-to heat treat blade in it
to coat the steel. Also available is a foil used to wrap
the blade. Either of these methods help prevent scale
and withstand the normalizing and heat treat cycles,
making for a fast and easy clean up after hardening. I
do not use either, because I feel the scale is easily

removed during the final grinding, but it is an option you may wish to consider.

The next time you raise the steel to this austenizing point, you want to cool it fast enough to freeze the carbon atoms within the cubes of iron. Most of the time this will be done by quenching in oil preheated to about 120°F, though some lower carbon steels will need a brine (salt water) quench to be cooled fast enough to harden. We are only dealing with simple steel here, so we will not be addressing air hardening or high alloy steels.

Not all oils are the same. Some are better than others, so please research before you buy. Using automatic transmission fluid (ATF) and motor oils will work. I used them in the beginning, but science has progressed a lot since many of the earlier books were written about blade making, and we smiths need to be aware of the new research if we wish to get the best from our blades. Moving to one of the high grade commercially produced steel quenching oils by Parks or one of the other brands will be worth the effort.

A word of caution: some smiths advocate using dirty motor oil as a quenchant, thinking this somehow will add carbon and case harden the steel. This has been proven to be dangerous and false.

If the steel will not harden in the oil, then you may need to use a water quench. In fact I do not simply use water, but instead a brine solution, made by dissolving as much table salt as possible into the water. It also helps reduce vapor pockets if we add something to break the surface tension of the water, such as a squirt of dish washing liquid.

When quenching in any liquid, vapor pockets can form around the steel. Agitation in the form of a gentle up and down motion can break this vapor jacket and allow even cooling of the steel. Use a gentle up and down motion, not a side to side or any fast motion when quenching, this can lead to warping. When we oil quench there will be flame ups; submerging the blade and tang complete will minimize this. After the flame goes down, watch the surface of the oil; you will see convection causing a rippling effect. Then give it about 30 seconds more before removing from the quench.

This quenching creates another form of steel known as martensite, where the carbon is trapped in a tetragonal crystal. This is the hardest form steel can take, but it is also very brittle, so you must immediately temper this. These grains will line up in a lathe or plate form. I have had blades crack while waiting to temper. So warm the temper oven to the proper temperature before you start to harden and you should not have this problem.

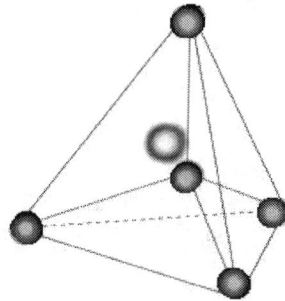

Tempering

Tempering relaxes the thermal shock caused during the hardening process. Most steels take a temper of only 325°F or so for a stress relief. I prefer a temper of 350°F when first out of the oil for two hours, a rest period of one day, and then a second temper at the correct temperature for the desired hardness for the steel used. When you harden the blade, there may be retained austenite, which is a small amount of the austenite that has not yet converted to martensite. This will convert into martensite after some time at room temperature.

To make sure you do not have any untempered martensite in your blade, wait a full day before giving your blades a second tempering cycle. This is a reason many use a subzero quench for advanced steel treatment. It forces the change into martensite in high alloy steels, but does not do much for lower alloy steels.

Using a higher tempering temperature will result in a softer blade that takes more beating before breaking but reduces the edge retention. As with your steel choices, it is all a compromise and there is no one size fits all.

Tempering temperature is best checked with a thermometer. But long ago observing the temper colors was the only method available, and is still being used today. These colors are a result of the oxides that form on the surface of the polished metals which increase in thickness as temperature rises. As the layer of oxides get thicker, it reflects different colors.

This is a very predictable method for each steel type. Use the chart at the beginning of this chapter, or the full color print on the rear cover, as a guide only. The color I see at 400°F you may be starting to see at 375°F. Also be aware that the ambient lighting will effect the way the colors appear, as will the color be different for different steel alloys.

Advanced Thermal Treatments

Now and then we see information passed down once again about how stainless steel cannot match the awesome carbon steel in a knife blade. While I do not use stainless steel very often, I have nothing against using it.

Unless the maker of any knife blade has a shop testing protocol that will assure he or she is getting the proper heat treat proper for that individual steel, what alloy is used will not matter.

This also applies to mystery steels. If the maker is a bladesmith with the understanding to determine whether the steel is worthy of the efforts needed to make a blade, he or she can indeed make a fine knife.

Something strongly in favor of simple steels for a blade is that someone with the ability to manage a fire and forge with a minimum of heats, and not over heat or forge too cool can craft a blank that may become a knife.

Simple high carbon steels can be hardened and tempered properly in most home shops. All of these things stack the odds in favor of a blade that works as intended if the smith works as he or she should. Also any omissions in the process will not work out well.

Always keep a log book on what you do in the heat treating process. The log provides a reference on what worked on the various types of steels, so the next time you do it, you will not have to spend time figuring it out again. You can just repeat what you did the last time you used that steel.

Stainless Steel

Stainless is different for a few reasons. I only know of a few that can be forged without cracking in the process. There might be more. Some may be hardened and tempered in some advanced home shops.

Most stainless steels suitable for blade work require a hardening process that is atmospherically controlled and done at rather exacting temperatures that are hard to reach and maintain for the time necessary in a home shop. To properly harden will take a many hour soak time. After hardening, wait for the stainless steel to cool to room temperature then perform a subzero quench. Many stainless steels need this procedure to force conversion of the retained austenite.

Subzero Quenching

I will present the following for informational purposes only. Another thermal process is called subzero quenching. When hardening, not all of the austenite converts to martensite during the quench. This leftover austenite is called "retained austenite" and will usually, or at least partly, convert given a long enough time. The purpose of a subzero quench is to force this conversion of austenite into martensite in a much shorter amount of time, allowing us to get the metal tempered, rather than allowing it to remain as the brittle untempered martensite after it gets converted on its own much later.

This is mostly applicable to high alloy steels, but some low alloy steels may benefit from a home shop process. Only testing will prove if this is true. The home freezer is not cold enough to do much, though a process involving crushed dry ice and acetone can result in a temperature drop to about -170 °F, while a quench with liquid Nitrogen will result in a drop to about -300°F and is used for many stainless steels.

In the home method, crush dry ice and place in a container, along with the blade. Pour acetone into the container, and leave the blade to get cold to convert some of the retained austenite into martensite. Never add dry ice to the acetone; it can explode if you do it that way. This process can be volatile, including explosions, so take proper precautions, including thick gloves and protective clothing. Do not allow the metal to contact any bare skin, or you may lose that skin. Remove the blade after 30 seconds, then allow it to reach room temperature.

Either method requires a tempering cycle to address the newly formed martensite. Most high carbon stainless steels that are right for knives require a hardening process that is atmospherically controlled and done at rather exacting temps that are hard to reach and hold for the time necessary in a home forge. You must wear gloves and use tongs, also be sure to wear face protection and long sleeves. I hope you can understand why I rarely choose to use stainless, and when I do, I prefer to use a professional heat treater to do the job.

Triple Normalizing

Previously I touched on triple normalizing to refine grain. This is a variation for refinement by using temperature control to get even finer grains in our steel.

In this process, start at a point about 150°F above the curie temperature of the steel in question for your normalizing. After allowing it to cool, take the steel to a point about 100°F above the curie point. Allow to cool a third time and take the steel to a point about 50°F above. This thermal cycling by 50°F steps causes the grain boundaries to reform again, which is similar to other triple normalizing processes. But by reducing the target temperature by 50°F each time, you are now avoiding the same grain growth before being cycled again. This lower temperature cycling creates somewhat smaller grains than you would have created if you cycled from the same temperatures each time.

Many alloy steels have other qualities that may, at times, work in our favor. Carbide precipitation of Fe_3C, can be used with good effect in the form of alloy banding or carbide banding. While most metallurgists work very hard to avoid this in their steels, blade makers can exploit this for the medieval Damacus or Wootz-type effect on the surface of some higher alloy steels, such as the alloy D2. A mild acid bath, such as used with pattern welding can assist in accentuating this effect.

Differential Hardening

There is another class of hardening that is called differential hardening, where you only harden the cutting edge portion of the blade, leaving the spine tougher and more flexible.

When making a Japanese Katana, a clay is used to mask off the spine of the blade, creating a heat sink which slows the cooling for that portion of the steel when quenched, thus preventing the formation of martensite beneath the clay.

The blade curves a bit after this rapid quench, resulting in the traditional curve of these blades, and creates a band of pearlite along the border where the clay was placed.

Pearlite is a two-phased layered structure composed of alternating layers of alpha-ferrite (88 wt%) and cementite (12 wt %).

This edge formations is known as a Hamon. See photo 25 of a Japanese style blade by Rick Barrett for an extreme example of what can be achieved.

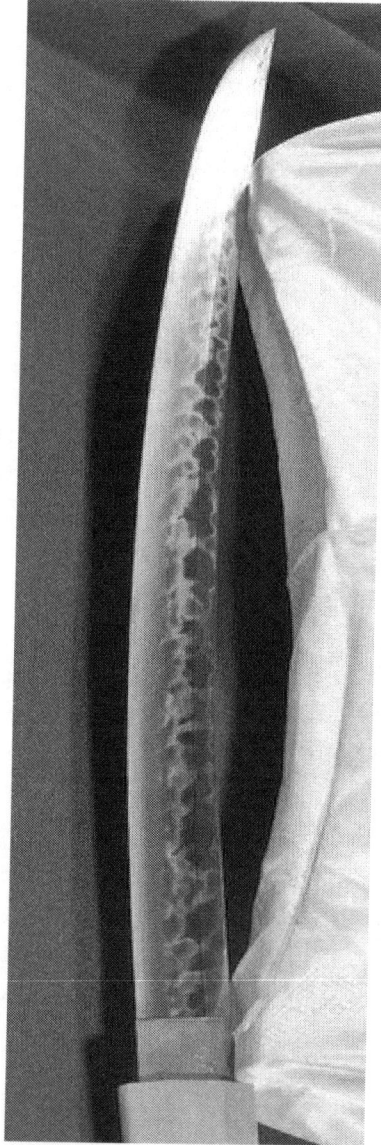

Illustration 25: Japanese styled blade by Rick Barret.

Notice the details in the cloud like features, called Yakiba, in this Hamon. This is the result we all dream of achieving.

One can "edge quench" where only the cutting edge and a small fraction of the blade are immersed in the quenchant, but this method usually results in a Hamon that is rather plain. Edge quenching will never result in the beautiful elaborate patterns seen in photo number 25.

Whichever method you chose to use in making your blade hard enough to be a knife, you should follow the process with at least a short tempering cycle to relieve stress.

Along these same line is a process called "differential tempering". While you still temper the entire blade, this procedure requires you draw the spine even more. For example, if you draw the temper color to a soft gold (380°F) on the cutting edge but want more flex in your blade, you can use a heated iron, plate, or even small tip torch; to heat only the spine to a blue color (500°F). This is much easier to do if you place the cutting edge in water while heating the back. This is very nice as it gives the option of a blade that is tough as a blue temper would be, but with the cutting edge of a gold temper on the same blade. A blue temper for the entire blade would not hold the same type of edge for long because it would be too soft.

Salt tanks have become popular in recent years, due in part to the efforts of Professor Bain, as well as Howard Clark. I will not go into details of salt tanks here, as that is a subject for advanced blade makers. It also has a higher risk of danger if mistakes are made. I will state that special salts are used to heat and cool the steel being treated. These salts are not common table salts, and any moisture on the blade upon entering the salt can result in an explosion as water turns into steam, rapidly expanding about 1600 times in volume. But these are perfect for creating "bainite", Professor Bain originally described this as being similar in appearance to tempered martensite. A fine, non-layered structure, bainite commonly consists of cementite and dislocation-rich ferrite and has a needle like grain. The high concentration of dislocations in the ferrite present in bainite makes this ferrite harder than it normally would be. Bainite has a hardness between pearlite and martensite.

Salts offer very fine temperature controls, and as such are also used for "austempering", "marquenching" and various other methods that are beyond the scope of a simple book like this one.

Tangs

After the basic heat treat process is finished I use an Oxyacetylene torch to heat the tang to a very dull red while the blade portion is submerged in water. This prevents affecting the temper of the blade's cutting edge. This high temperature tempering of the tang makes it as soft as possible while also keeping it in the martensetic structure. Metallurgists call this a differential temper, leaving one section harder than another. I also use this same hand torch procedure on larger blades to make the spine softer by holding the cutting edge in the water and using the torch on the spine.

I am aware that some blade makers advocate not hardening the tang at all. I disagree with this. I feel that if I were not to harden the tang when I did the initial hardening, it would create a dramatic line of demarcation between the austenite and martensite structures, potentially creating stress, which is subject to breaking at that point later.

Now that the tang has been made very soft, I trim and shape the tang to the desired profiles, thinning the tang to its own proximal taper, so it is not bulky, but has a more graceful taper. I also drill pin holes for the handle material pins. I only finish the sides of a tang with 40 grit as I want it rough to better hold the glues.

Consistency

When it comes to its intended ability to cut, slice, chop, etc., a blade of any material may be a wonderful thing or just scrap metal in spite of how it looks or feels. We must avoid overheating the steel to keeping the metals properties intact during shaping and the entire heat treat process as well. Follow up testing and applying of the correct edge geometry and support is the heart of a good blade. I do not care if it is your first blade or you have made hundreds. If you make the blade correctly it will be correct.

When I hear that any steel has a bad reputation for blades, I first wonder if that was a steel alloy that could be adapted for use as a blade. When I hear that someone has a preference for a particular kind of steel I think of how nice it is they have found a steel that has been properly prepared in all the ways that make that happen for them. And I say this without regard to who is the maker.

I hope that anyone that makes knives and reads this will follow testing protocols and see how their work holds up to simple shop tests. Harden a blade-sized piece of steel and break it safely; look at the grain structure. Then make a blade from the same steel and do all of the steps in heat treat. Fashion a blade and test it, using bending tests, cutting tests, chopping tests, etc.

For blade testing, there is no need to spend a lot of time on fittings and handles for this; just use something that makes the blade usable.

Remember to do this all again when you change steels, and if you record all the data, you can likely repeat the result in the future if you know which steel you are using.

Earlier I covered hardening steel. In addition, there are a few other ways we can use heat to make changes to our steels internal structure.

Excessive heat can cause the grains to grow to a point where an otherwise fine blade steel is unusable. If it has not been burned, we can use various techniques to get our grains small again.

In the past there was an erroneous term for a mythical process called "edge packing," which was a method used to get the grain smaller. The theory was that hammering steel colder than normal forging temperatures would shatter the grains to get them smaller. This is a partially false assumption.

Steel grains do not pack, and most anything we do as to grain size in our forging is wiped out during the final heat treating anyway, so long as we do not allow the grains to grow overly large. But lower temperature forging at the end does result in a smother surface on our work.

Quality Control

No matter what we buy, there can be unknown additions to the steel due to the modern manufacturing process, as well as the substitution some suppliers make when they run out of a given product. We all have our own equipment, which may not be as accurate as the testing labs that make the charts. So our temperatures can be off.

Getting to know the properties of our chosen steel can aid us in getting better blades. Remember that the spec sheets temps and soak times are for a 1 inch thickness. In blade work we are dealing with much thinner sections.

First, harden using the manufacturers recommended temperature. For this example, I will use 1550°F. After hardening test this steel; you do not need a blade, because only thickness matters. Now break and examine the grain. Then harden another the exact same way at 1500°F, then a third at 1600°F. You may have to do a few more tests at various temperatures, but compare what hardening temperature change alone does to this thickness of steel. Also feel free to allow a the steel to rest at this temperature, known as a soak, to this thin steel, and compare.

Testing like this, or in similar ways, is the only way to decide if you should soak your steel or not before you quench. I think you will find most simple steels do not need a soak. In fact, many will have pronounced grain growth from the extra heat. This way you can discover the exact perfect temperature for this batch of steel.

Straightening

Occasionally we will have a blade warp during the heat treating process. Wearing gloves, we can sometimes correct this by hand, as we have until the blade cools to about 400°F before it sets up, and gets hard and brittle.

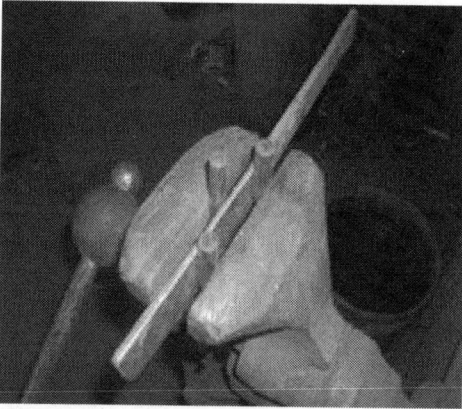

Illustration 26: Straightening a warp.

If gentle hand adjustment does not correct the warp, before it gets to room temperature, place it in a vise that has three rods attached to the jaws. Two rods are on one jaw with a gap between them. The remaining rod is placed on the opposing jaw, centered between the first two. Gentle pressure when closing the vise jaws will correct the warp if not too drastic a bend, nor too cold. If in doubt, anneal and straighten hot, then try the heat treating process again, because you only have a short time after hardening before it "sets." After that, you can crack the blade, bending it like this.

Chapter 5

Grinding

A belt grinder uses easily changeable belts to grind away metal. These belts can get clogged with debris and no longer remove material as they should. To clean the abrasives I use an eraser type that knife suppliers sell as a belt cleaner.

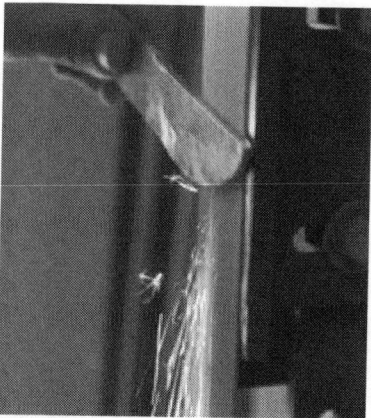

Illustration 27: Knocking off square edges.

When you put a square edge to a belt it removes grit as it works, more so than a rounded or less sharp edge. Grind that edge back with the blade edge down, as in photo 27. This will also help protect belts from tearing.

To get more life from a grinding belt, flip it over after you think the belt is worn too much, and you can get a little more work out of it. Generally it is best to forget the cost of belts when using them and replace them as needed.

Finishing

You need to take care not to remove too much material from the blade before heat treat. I rough grind and leave a cutting edge the thickness of a dime. This leaves enough material to ensure I can remove the outer layer that has lost some carbon due to the heat, called the decarb zone, and have a good solid blade after heat treating.

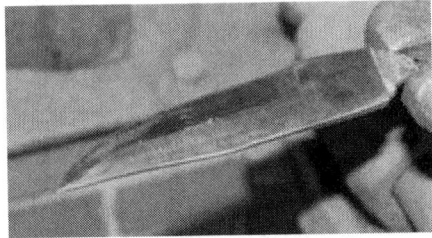

Illustration 28: Blade after edge bevel has been ground.

In order to get a clean mirror polish on a knife blade, I use an old 220 grit blue Ceramic belt after the heat treat. Then use a 400 grit yellow Klingspor or a Norzon 30 micron belt, finishing with 15 and maybe even a 9 micron belt. The 30 micron is similar to a 400 grit, 15 is similar to a 700 grit, and 9 micron is close to 1200 grit. I hand sand with 1500, 2000 and 3000 grit Silicon Carbide papers, depending on how far I want to go. For the handles and scales I have Aluminum Oxide belts for the machine; then I finish by hand sanding.

Experiment with the way you work to find what grits and types of belts you prefer. When I first got my 2 x 72 machine I asked the supplier for an assortment of grits and types so I could see what worked best with my methods.

One of the keys to getting a smooth consistent grind on a blade is to apply even pressure to the blade as it is held against the grinding wheel. Use a push stick made from scrap wood for even pressure.

Illustration 29: My push stick.

Illustration 30: Push stick on the 10 inch contact wheel.

Make sure the wheel is at the correct height for the operator. The push stick should have the blade held firmly, and your knees should have enough bend to allow your body to move from side to side as you grind the blade. Lock your hands against your belly and make sure they stay there; movement should occur from the whole body. If your hands get away from your belly, you will lose control of the blade and will not keep the lines correct.

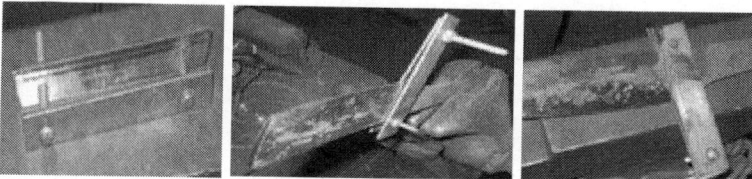

Illustration 31   Close up of grinding jig.

The trio of pictures in figure 31, show a jig you can use to help you keep the bevel of the blade even. Grind lines look better when they are even side to side, and square to the edges. This is simply a clamp made of scrap steel. It is 5 inches long, 3/16 inch thick, and has been drilled for 1/4-20 bolts to hold it in position. Grind the inner sides of the clamp with 400 grit to prevent scratching the blade. The advantage of this mounting system is that the angles of the blade can be matched by tightening one side more than the other for a close fit.

This can assist you to get good bevels. Even with the many years experience I have making blades, I still use files to get the clean lines for the transition of the knife bevel to the choil. I also tend to use over long pieces of steel so my hands do not get too hot, and I can use my hands to hold the blade as long as possible.

Grit Selection

Now we will look at the blade as it is ground with the different belts. I leave all of my blades a little on the thick side so I can flatten out any warping that may be caused by the heat treat, as well as remove the decarb zone in the process. All my blades have been rough ground to 220 grit prior to heat treat. Afterwards I grind the blades with a used 120 grit belt to remove any scale from the heat treat process. The new ones are a bit too sharp for this task.

The goal with this belt is to establish all the lines. Both grinds should start at the same place on each side of the blade. The top line of the hollow grind should be the same across the top and end at the same place on each side of the blade.

This photo shows the blade after grinding with a 120 grit belt. See the dark pits in the edge of the blade, this is left over from forging. I must remove these before changing belts.

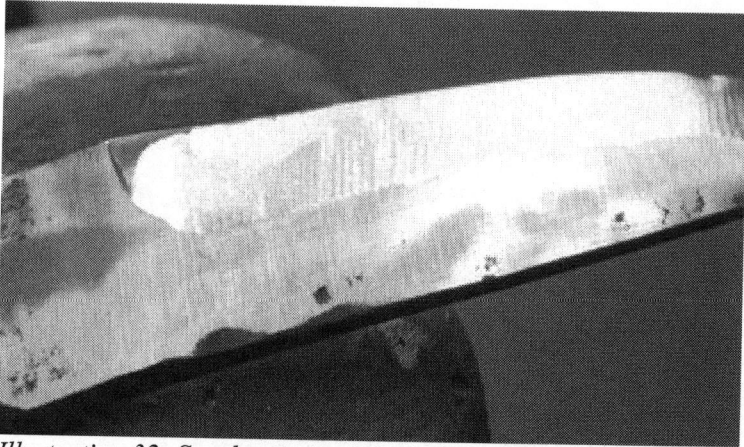

Illustration 32: See the pits in this rough ground blade?

Look closely at this blade, and you will see a nice even lines where the side ends and the bevel begins. These lines will round over and come out blurry if I am not careful.

I hope you noted that for all of the work with the belt grinder I have held the blade with the edge up and used the push stick, keeping my hands firmly close to my belly and moving side to side for the grind. When you are sure you have all the lines correct, all the scratches removed and the blade is a nice satin finish from the 15 micron belt, it is almost time to hit the buffer. But first let's test the blade.

Testing

Before we buff the blade to perfection, we must first make sure it is a quality knife and not just a "knife shaped object." Perform these tests to find out whether you have a quality blade. The edge must hold its sharpness.

Start with a flex test by placing the blade edge at an angle against a ½ inch diameter rod. Press to see if the blade start to move with that curve, then release to

Illustration 33: Angle of edge flex test.

see if it returns to its beginning position. Check in 3 or 4 places then check the edge by shaving a little hair from your arm. If the blade does not shave, you must repeat the heat treat process, making adjustments to correct the problem. If this turns out as you wish, then you have a quality edge. It will flex a little rather than break, and also will return to shape after the flexing.

To see if the blade holds up to use, chop up some fire wood or half a section of 2x4 pine stud. Check the shaving ability again after cutting through the lumber. You could place a stack of paper or cardboard in the vise, and cut sections. It works about the same as using the wood, so use what you prefer.

Some smiths have purchased a Rockwell tester. This is wonderful machine. The machine uses a pointed tool-to press into the steel edge and measures the depth of penetration, assigning that depth a number. For blades we use the Rockwell Hardness "C" or "RhC," scale. Most blades should be between 50 to 62 RhC. Note the Rockwell tester does not return a meaningful number with pattern welded steels due to the thinness of each different layer giving a different reading, even on the same blade. Because of this problem, I prefer the Rockwell testing files, which are a series of files marked with the resistance range relating to the hardness of the steel being tested.

Every so often make what is called a test blade, especially when getting a new batch of steel or making a change to the current process of creating blades for any reason. This blade will get abused. It has been made for the sole purpose of destroying it. I will chop fire wood and phone books, and eventually I place the blade in a vise, bending it over 90 degrees cold, to see how my blade holds up to hard abuse.

Always wear a face/neck shield and other personal protection equipment while preforming these tests. I suggest you use either a pipe or welding glove over the blade to contain the pieces when the blade breaks. This is a great way to find out how well your pattern welded blades are, as you can see inside the break and examine the welds, and grain structure of the steel.

Most people will not abuse a blade like this, but some have used blades as a can opener, or a pry bar, or screw driver. So you want to see what will happen to your blades if they fail to be sure of no one getting hurt by a shattered blade. You also want to make sure a blade holds up under normal use keeping its edge a very long time.

In Addition

I prefer using 10xx series and L-6 grade steels for making blades. I have also used other steels such as W-2, 5160 and O-1 and even some some very advanced steels. However, except for when I use 440C stainless steel as part of a pattern welded mix, I send all my stainless steels to a commercial heat treating place, and strongly suggest you do too. For non stainless steels, such as O1, L-6,W2, 1095 and others, I do all the heat treating in my shop.

Buffing

After you have proven to yourself this piece of metal is worthy of being called a knife, clean up any marks from the testing and polish.

For buffing, work without the push stick, but keep your hands on your belly for support like you did with the grinding phase to get the best control. Keep your knees bent for movement, buffing with the knife edge held down. Only put the part of the blade against the wheel that is on the floor side of the blade. For the upper part of the blade, turn the blade and work once again towards the floor on the part of the blade nearest the floor. You do not want the buff to come over the top edge of the blade as you work, or it will try and remove the blade from your hands.

My machine is set up with 6 inch buffs. I prefer using the white diamond buffing compound for a mirror finish, but some prefer the green chrome oxide which is about 0.5 micron. I also have black Emery and brown Tripoli on hand for satin blades. Whatever you choose to use is up to you. While buffing, you must not switch between buffs and/or compounds without a full cleaning of the blade. Use one compound per buffing wheel. Changing a compound means also changing a wheel. While working, you must clean the blade before moving to another buffing wheel to avoid cross contamination.

To set up the buffing process, use the same steps taken earlier with the belts. For a blade of about four inches, you can buff both sides and finish up in less than 3 or 4 minutes. If you find scratches that do not come out right away, return to the grinder and use a 15 micron to remove them. Examine closely, and if they are gone, go back to the buff. If the scratches are still there try a 30 micron, until you find where you cleaned the courser lines then move to the 15 micron again. When all scratches are gone and the blade has a nice shine, buff again. If you follow through and do not skip over cleaning up all of the scratches, you can make your blade almost glow.

The biggest key to a superior finish is in the quality control that you do. If you examine any blade under a microscope you will find lines so small that they cannot be seen by the naked eye. The lines will be of an even space and depth. Any lines that are not parallel or deeper than the rest will stick out. Yes, even small lines that are not like the rest show up with normal vision.

Do you want or need to put a mirror polish on your blades? That is your call. These methods not only apply to blades, but also to anything you make or restore. It will work on anything you want to polish, including natural or man-made handle materials.

Types of Buffing Compounds

Choose carefully what you put on the buffing wheel. Some of the black emery compounds are about 400 grit. If you go as fine as a 9 micron, remember it is around 1800 grit, and you will put in scratches with the buffer and a 400 grit emery compound. Match the grit of the belts and the grade of compound with the finish you desire.

I believe some knife blades look really nice with a finish done with 220 grit belts. However, it will suffer if you buff it with the fine compounds as it will get blotchy and uneven. A 15 micron belt gives a nice shine without the high polish and looks really nice. A compound around 1200 grit would work well with that. Try what you have in the shop and see what works and what fails.

Use the same series of belts and a smaller buffing wheel of around 4 inches diameter for handle work, I am using an old one that wore down from its prior size. I use the fine white compound on that wheel. The small size reduces the speed, and the white does not stain the material.

If you are working with high carbon steel, wipe the steel dry when you are not working on it. Carbon steel will rust right before your eyes if you let it, especially with the coarser grades of paper.

You can finish a blade with similar grits of wet or dry sanding paper wrapped over a flat metal piece. Work within the guidelines presented in this chapter and you should get the finish you like. Keep the paper wet as you work. A touch of dish soap in the water will keep the grit from clogging the paper.

Knives do not cut well if the edge is ground or polished too fine. In order to cut properly it needs some "tooth." I use 1,200 grit for the edge. While there are 8,000 grit stones available, and those are great for traditional medieval blade polishing on the edges, I feel it is much too fine and tends to result in an edge that cuts poorly.

Chapter 6

Bolsters

Preparation

Bolsters and guards are decorative and sometimes functional transitions between the blade itself and the handle you hold. Not all blade styles require having either bolsters or guards, but when you choose to use them, there are additional steps you need to take.

Rough file the edges around the tang to make sure you have the guard aligned correctly with the blade. Use a square along the spine. File until there is no gap on either side of tang. I use a chain saw file.

The point where the tang meets the ricasso is a likely point for a crack if you leave a square inside corner. This is a potential stress riser, which is a place where stress from normal use compounds and may result in a break. Take a little round needle file and remove that corner. You may want to file into the tang a little bit so there is no longer a sharp corner.

Making a Guard

Many people slot guards with a milling machine; however, if you are like me and do not have one, then make do and use what you have. Here in picture 34 you can see how I took a piece of steel and forged a slitter. It is sized so it would not cut a hole bigger than the tang. The tip is a little rounded and the end kind of like a square point.

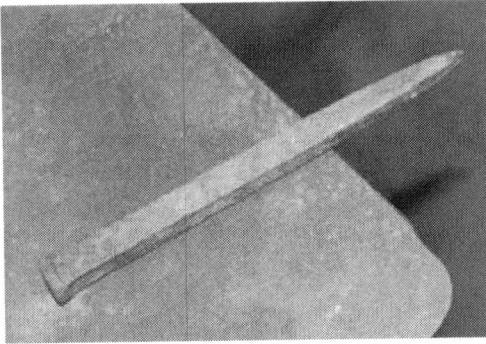

Then I forged another slitter very close to the size of the tang both width and thickness. I used a 3/4" x 1" piece of mild steel for the guard.

Illustration 34: Slitter.

Mark where you want the slot and use the slitter with light taps to make sure the slot is straight. There is no need to heat treat either of these tools. The heat from the steel will destroy any effects from a heat treat anyway.

After marking the spot, get the guard steel hot and punch a hole with the slitter you made.

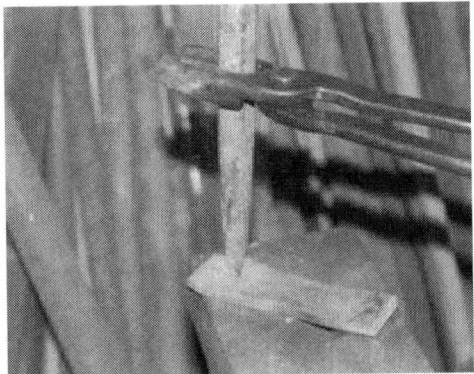

Illustration 35: Beginning the slot.

Put the guard back into the fire to bring it up to working heat, and let the slitter cool. Place the guard material over the hardy hole again continuing to drive the slitter through the guard. When it pops out the back side, tap the guard off and cool the tool. Straighten the guard and reheat. You will have to do the same process a little from the other side, as well. This will widen the bar of steel as you are moving metal not removing it. And that is good because you need the guard a little wider than the size we started with at first.

Now heat and flatten the guard out; leave no hammer marks on either side. The other tool that you forged a little smaller than the tang is to be used as a drift. Heat the bar and run the drift in from one side then the other. Forge the end a little more to get the steel like you want for the guard.

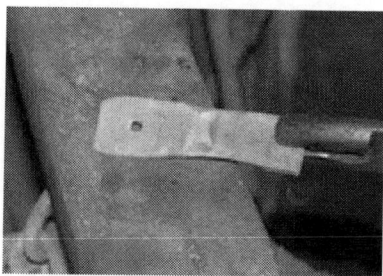

Illustration 36: Punched.

Also work the other side of the slot a little. You want to do some of this shaping before cutting the guard away from the larger bar. It is easier to put in and out of the forge when you have this built-in handle. After the heat treat clean up the blade with abrasives as necessary. Then use small files to finally fit this guard. When you are happy with the finish on the metal, you can use a product called JB Weld® around the tang instead of solder.

Some people do not want to solder. Make sure as the JB Weld® dries, you clean it off as it squeezes out at the guards joint at the tang. You can cut the end of a Popsicle® stick into a wedge to do scrape it clean. If you do not seal this joint moisture can enter and cause rust.

Forge the tang, then put the hole in the guard while the blade is in the tempering oven. You have to work with what technology you have available for your own set-up. Your brain is your best tool.

Attaching Bolsters

Bolsters are not hard to make or install. However, if you want a nice fit and finish follow these steps. They may seem complicated but will save you time. The area where the bolster will be, needs at least 2 holes. In picture 37, I am using three holes, drilled and chamfered before heat treat. I rough cut some 3/16 inch thick stainless steel for the bolsters. I will complete the final shaping of these bolsters after mounting the bolsters solidly in place.

I do not have to worry about the finish changing over time because I used the same grade of stainless steel for both the pins and for the bolsters, I now have rough cut over size bolsters, I clamped the first bolster in place for drilling the first hole.

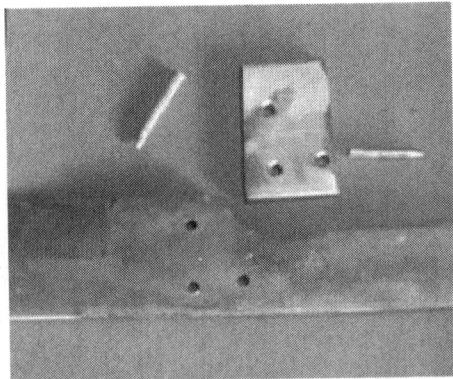

Illustration 37: Setting up for bolsters.

Photo 37 also shows a pair of long pins that are tapered at one end. To get this taper, use a drill press to make a hole and put in one pin with the end flattened. That keeps it from falling onto the floor while we drill the other holes. Remove the clamp if needed, then drill and pin the rest. Then drill the other side.

Make marks with a Sharpie® or soap stone on the top and bottom of the blade and bolster before removing the first bolster so you can line the second bolster up when it is drilled. Check and see if all pins pass through easily with the others in place. Recheck the finish on both sides of the blade and the front of the guard.

Illustration 38: Pins in place.

Make sure everything lines up well. Smooth the sides of both bolsters where they meet the blade with 120 grit. Then countersink the holes on that side. This allows the pin to get a head set into the bolster where it will hold, and not be seen. You do not want a sharp edge to shave any metal from a pin. Put both bolsters on and drop in the pins. If a hole is tight drill right through. These pins are not precision fit.

Then nip off the ends of the 1/8" pins with nippers, leave a little for peening. I use one and a half times the diameter, so a 1/8 inch pin gets 3/16 inch, a ¼ inch pin would need 3/8 length on each side. I use about a 16 oz ball peen and work one side then the other so the pin stays centered as it mushrooms over both sides. Having a plate with a small divot helps hold the head of the mushroom. Tap around so the two bolsters stay tight to the blade. After they are flattened down we are ready for the next step.

You may see a line on top and bottom of the bolsters, where they meet the blade, as in this photo. If you do, you need to close the gap. Lay them on the anvil and support the other side; hit the top side several times to tighten that seam at the blade to bolster contact point.

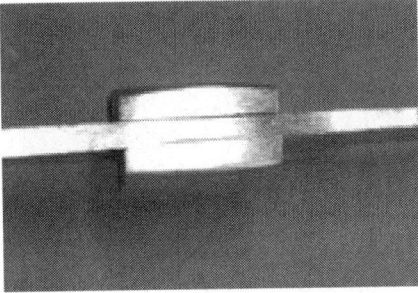

Illustration 39: Check for gaps.

Flatten both sides on top and bottom of the bolster. This will be clearer soon. Now use the belt grinder and dress both sides. You want these to taper, thicker where the scales meet and a little thinner at the ricasso, a 120 grit belt works well for this. When you get them both rough dressed so there are no more flat spots, look and see if they are same thickness at the handle end and ricasso end. A variance under .002 inch is good.

Illustration 40: Rough profiles for bolsters.

Making this next style requires you to be cutting a slot for a cross guard common to many swords and large knives. On page 88, I already showed how you pierce the guard and make a rectangular hole for passing the tang. To do this you will use the drill press. First get the guard to rough shape. In this case it is blocky only to show what to do. Also a block is easier to hold in a vise to work.

Mark off where you want the slot. This hole is intended to be smaller than what we want the finished hole to be.

Drill out a few holes to get the material out of the way. Then, using either hand files or a flex shaft

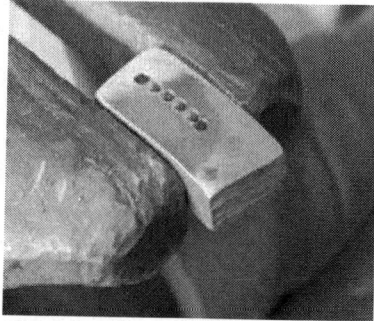

Illustration 41: Drilled slot to be cut.

tool, remove the rest as shown in photo 42. Now you should have a squared hole that is a little too tight for the tang. Carefully open the hole with files to fit perfectly so it fits on the tang , and it will not wobble in use.

As you make this you will not have a perfect parallel

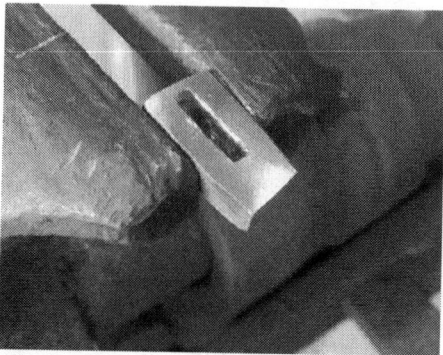

Illustration 42: Slot cut.

cut, because the tang has a slight taper, the hole must match that. That is another reason to make the hole undersized. If you do this correctly there is no need for solder to hold it in place, but I still solder it to keep the moisture out.

I have used pattern welded material, wrought iron, brass, bronze, and nickel silver to make the guards. Most of these materials work about the same way. Copper and brass look good at first. But then they oxidize and look different. If the new owner knows this can happen, he or she may maintain them and keep the copper and brass looking great.

Illustration 43: Soldering the guard in place.

Slotted Guards

To prepare for this type of guard, a full tang blade has to have a slot cut before heat treat. There are several things to see in the picture 44. The bottom of the blade is notched before the heat treat.

You can use a mill, but, I drill a hole in the guard and use a hacksaw and file to properly size the hole. I have a 3/8 inch thick guard and have cut a notch to fit the thickness of my blade.

Illustration 44: Guard solidly in place.

Note that I have slightly closed the end of the guard, then tapered the inside of that slot at the open end so it would start on the blade and then be tapped in place and not move.

Now that all is fit properly, polish the flat sides of the blade to the final finish including the little area on the bottom of the ricasso between the hollow grind and the guard and the front of the guard. You cannot get to those places once you solder the guard in place. Then take a flex shaft with a disk, and clean out the inside of the blade notch. I used a round needle file to remove the square corners in the notch to eliminate stress risers.

Many bowies have a slotted guard, that slips into place from the tang end rather than over the tang. You mark another bar for making the guard, drill the starting hole, use a saw to file away the remainder, so the guard slides into place on the blade.

Recheck all surfaces in bright light and polish if needed. Then tap the guard in place and make sure it is square with the blade and cannot be twisted out of plumb.

Be sure to solder this guard on the back, the tang side. Otherwise you will have a visible line on the back side of the guard when you finish it. Leave the guard long enough to extend over the spine of the blade a little bit. You can remove the excess later. Solder the area where the slots of the guard touches the spine of the blade, to eliminate lines when finished.

Then solder the area on both sides of the point where guard and ricasso meet. Use no-lead plumbing solder and the flux that comes with it. A flux brush helps because if you lay on too much solder, you can brush the solder away so clean up takes less time. It will take you a few times to get the solder right. It is not unusual to take the guard back off, re-clean and polish it and attach it again. That is a short version on how to do this style guard.

I did not recess the guard in the tang, only on the edge. Cutting into the tang could make a weak spot in the tang so form the slot in the bolster to fit the tang. Any sharp transition will be a stress riser, where the stress will focus and may cause a failure later.

I use stainless steel, pure nickel or bronze for these kinds of guards. For using mild steel, try gun browning or gun bluing for the guard. Lots of folks use brass for guards, butt caps and pins. I have used it in the past but rarely do anymore. If you go to gun shows that have knives or knife shows, you will see a wide range of knives displayed for sale. Often but not always, the lower end knives will have brass fittings. While mirror polished brass looks really nice that polished look fades quickly. It is not easier to work than nickel, however nickel is pricey. I think bronze has a lot of good things for new makers, such as the following:

- Easier to work.
- Looks really good when done right.
- Lets you complete a knife in less time than if you use stainless or even mild steel.

I have used lost wax casting to cast a bronze guard so nice it needed almost no fitting or finishing. However, you can drill file and fit a brass guard in less time, but then you have a brass guard that does not age as nicely as bronze. There are many levels of fit and finish to work through as you learn and progress. The better materials and the nicer fit and finish are what makes the price go up.

Start at the beginning. Determine at what level you can work at. If you are new then start simple stock removal guards. If you are already forging blades well, try fancy forged designs for guards. Do what suits how you work and your comfort level.

Chapter 7

Handles

Tangs

The tang is the section of the blade where the handle is attached. It needs to absorb the stress put on the blade in use, the impact of a chopper, or steady pressures in slicing. Some blades use a rat tail tang, which is not very strong, and is basically a small rod at the end of the blade. I was taught that it is best to have the tang as wide as possible to spread out the forces put on the blade.

Some of my knives are full tang knives and I taper the tang on them. I also cut into the blade a bit so a slotted guard slides tightly in place and then it is soldered.

For tapered tangs use stock removal. This also can be done on a forged blade. I use my belt grinder with a 10 inch wheel and hollow grind the tang. The alignment of the taper has to be to center to make the end of the tang correct. Use a scribe with a sharp carbide point that will scratch hardened steel.

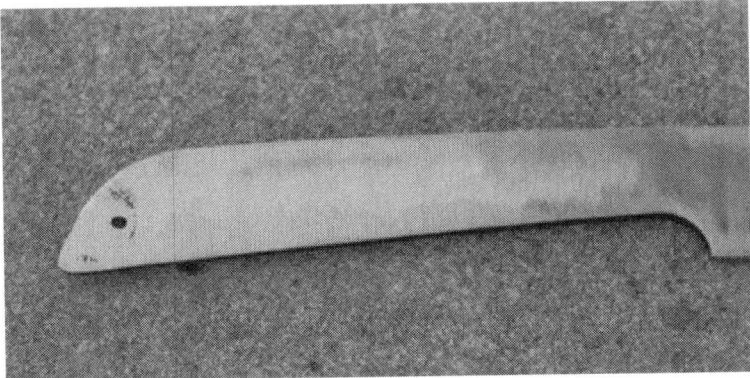

Illustration 45: Tang hollow ground for scales.

Blacken the tang area of the blade with a permanent marker. This works just as well as layout fluid, but costs much less. Scribe two lines showing how you want the tang and grind from each side down to those lines with a belt grinder. Hollow grind the entire tang just inside these lines up to the handle side of the guard.

Calipers are used to take measurements. The nice thing with these calipers is no matter how far you open them, the jaws remain parallel.

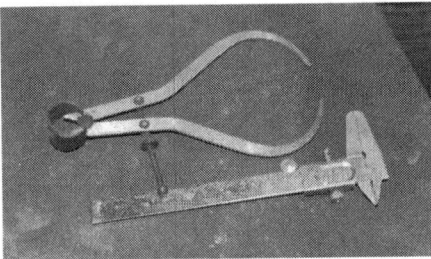

Illustration 46: Calipers.

Put in the tang, then hold up the knife to the light and see whether the edge's grind is flat and parallel. I use 120 grit for this. Check it along the tang's length. When all is flat, taper the other side of the tang and check this again to make sure.

Now that you have the guard in place and are ready for scales, grind the outside of the scales to rough fit the tang. Hollow grind the backs of the scales to assist in bonding. If you glue flat surfaces to flat surfaces you can clamp them together and most of the glue is squeezed out. This hollow grinding of the tang and scale backs makes room for epoxy.

One part of making a knife that can take a lot of time is smoothly blending the handle into the guard. You can use die grinders, rat tail files, half round files, carbide cutters in the drill press, or mandrel mounted abrasive wheels in a flex shaft. Often I make use of my small wheel attachments to my grinder (page 47, fig 20). This is a small bracket attachment for the grinder that allows access to tight places. I have 5/8" and 1" contact wheels. There are other sizes available for this.

When you are ready to grind a handle from its "as glued" state to a finished handle use a 120 grit belt to shape it. You must be careful with antler as you do not want to take anymore off of the face than you have to in order to fit. It is preferred to remove from the back (inside) of the antler, and other surface textured materials.

I recommend using calipers to check every so often and see that you are not getting out of line before it is too late to save your handle.

To make that perfect ricasso, I use the same flat grinder with all grits to polish the sides of the blades.

On the edge side of the blade put a mark with the marker. Put a thumb next to that line as you grind into the plunge cut area.

Handle Materials

When I assemble a knife, I do not put a piece together with anything that will not last a long time. No matter what it does in its new life. Sheep horn looks great and it makes a great handle, but it is made from the same thing as hair. If you set sheep horns outside for a time, they rot quickly. If that same horn was stabilized, it lasts nearly forever. This also applies to ivory, and most woods.

Stabilizing

You can buy your materials stabilized from many sources, or you can do it yourself. I suggest you get your material professionally stabilized when you purchase it. If you insist on doing it yourself, it can be messy, but however it gets done, it is the only real way to keep some woods from falling apart. For example, Red Mallee burl is a beautiful wood from Australia, bright red with many tight burls. Once I used non stabilized as a handle and it fell apart after about about 3 months after finishing the knife.

If you are stabilizing it yourself, get the handle material close to the size wanted and place in a vacuum chamber along with enough solution to cover the handle material. Close the chamber, draw a vacuum with a pump, and wait until all bubbling stops.

Release the vacuum and pressurize to about 2 atmospheres. Leave it there for a few hours before removing the handle material and allowing the resins time to set up. Some resins need to bake in an oven to cure. The remaining solution can be reused next time. One advantage of using the correct stabilizer is that, after drying, you can finish and have no need to seal the wood. It is already sealed from the inside, and leaves a lovely high gloss finish. Antler, horn and wood all benefit from stabilization. After stabilizing they can last as long or longer than the blade.

For the amount of mess, effort, and time it takes to stabilize materials, I prefer to have them professionally stabilized. It is your shop, so it is your choice.

Antler and horn are not always flat, but you can straighten most pieces by placing the antler in boiling water. After a few minutes the antler it will be soft, and you can place it in between a set of pressure plates to flatten before they cool and get hard again.

The plates can be simply a pair of 3/8 inch thick mild steel plates, that have a 3/8 inch hole drilled in each of the 4 corners to bolt them together. After removing the softened antler from the boiling water, place it between the plates. Gently squeeze them together with a vise stopping if you feel any excessive resistance.

Three inch long bolts act as guides that keep the plates lined up while tightening. After tightening, put some washers and nuts on the bolts to keep the plates together, then remove the assembly from the vise, leaving it open for other uses.

Water buffalo has been a long time favorite of many. Cow horn is a viable alternative, ask for it at slaughter houses, or rendering plants. Remove the solid tip area, and use that for boot knives. The thick side sections should be cut into strips for scales. Even the areas where it is very thin can be used as spacers.

Assembly

Just about anyone can make a knife. And anyone can spend too much or too little time on it. There are things you can do along the build that make a huge difference in how it comes out at the end.

The blade in this photo is a pattern-welded skinning knife. It has been forged to the shape of a pattern, filed, and heat treated, using all the steps listed.

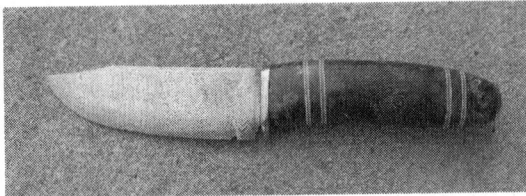

Illustration 47: Multi piece wood handle. Also shown on front cover of this book

Most everyone has the ability to use a block of wood and hand sand a blade. I admit it does take a long while. For less than $50 you can purchase a 1" x 30" grinder from a local box store. Use that until you sell enough blades to buy or build a pro-style 2"x72" machine.

At each step look close for large scratches you did not get out in the step before. After 600 grit I can take it right to the buffer. Look close for scratches and if you find a few, then go back to 400 grit and remove them, then 600 grit and then buff again. Note that this process does not hide anything. This extra time is needed for a nice blade.

Hidden Tangs

A word of warning: I sometimes use African Blackwood, which is a member of the rosewood family. It is naturally black with red and purple streaks throughout the grain. Like all other members of the rosewood group, it is very toxic to breathe the dust, so wear proper respiration protection.

The spacers and the handle pieces all have to be trued up. This will take time, but will be well worth the return. You can use an old farriers rasp. Clamp the rasp to your work bench, then move the pieces to smooth the sides. This is not the fun or easy part of making a nice handle. Each and every one of them has to have the sides parallel. Check the thickness with a caliper. All four sides have to be the same. When you are doing this, mark each piece with the silver pencil to mark what the thickness should be. The silver pencil shows up real well on this.

If using more than one section, use the rasp to get them to match in thickness. It is easier if you have a belt grinder with flat platen. When the sections are all the same move to the three pieces of wood for the handle, both end pieces have to match. The middle piece has to be true on each end, but can be shorter of longer. Measure all four sides and keep at it. From the rasp, move to using some 60 or 80 grit on all pieces to remove any roughness from rasping.

For this example, I had a skinning knife I need to mount and for this I used Buffalo Horn, with furniture of bronze I made of 90% copper and 10% tin. After casting the ingot, I forged down some pieces to get to the desired thickness for the guard, and the other sections I used. I wanted a thin separator so, rather than the Blackwood, I used 2 pieces of black vulcanized spacer material and nickel silver sheet between 2 sections of bronze.

After marking the spacers with a Sharpie©, I used the router drill bit in the drill press. For this tang I drilled two holes that were almost over lapping. Then I made the two holes meet by moving the horn in the right direction while the drill bit spun inside.

Do not push and break the drill. Be sure to wear eye protection. Repeat the process with the spacer materials. As they are smaller, you can hold them with a pair of pliers. When using pliers, if the drill bit catches, and spins the material, it can hurt you.

All the material is now drilled and marked. Use a little hammer and a block of wood to flatten them out again. At some point you have to measure all these spacers and the horn to make sure they are the correct length for this knife. This blade is 8" long with a 5" handle length. When you put it together, test fit to see that it is the correct length.

When you are cutting out these pieces, make sure you marked the top and one side. Mark arrows to show which way you want towards the guard with numbers one two and three so the grain will align like it was before being cut. Even with spacers in between the section of horn, your eyes follow that grain and will see if one is wrong. Your eyes will also see if any of the spacers are not parallel. Try for .002 inches or less within parallel.

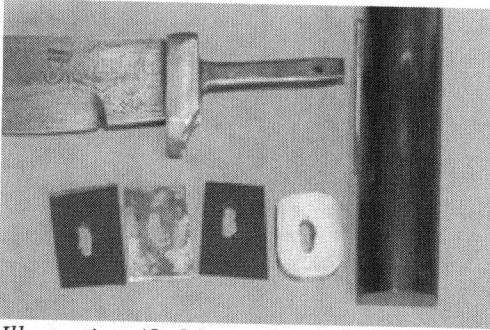

Illustration 48: Materials ready for assembly.

The drilled hole in the end of the tang was for the wire used to hang the blade while it cooled after the heat treating process. This tang has plenty of surface area for glue to hold the handle in place securely.

On the top left is the blade with bronze guard soldered in place. Below that is a section of black spacer material, nickel silver sheet, second black spacer, and the ¼ inch bronze. To the far right is the cylinder of buffalo horn to be used for the main body of the handl Use either clamps or rubber bands to hold the parts in place while the glues cure. Something to consider is that you do not want to crush the handle and squeeze out all of the glue. Rubber bands provide an ample amount of compression

Illustration 49: Partial guard assembly is glued up and held in clamps. Notice the blade showing on far right of photo.

with out crushing the handle. I use C clamps but remember to not make them too tight. It is also good to have some larger sizes for clamping, including some 48 inch long pipe clamps to put end pressure on long blades and scabbards.

Avoid the fast setting epoxy resins. They tend to fail after about 5 years. You can use almost anything, including resins, but most things will still need about 24 hours to cure, so why rush?

Knife suppliers have been through all of the epoxy brand's and usually stopped carrying those that do not work out in long run. They have all the epoxy, glues, etc. that work well, so they are a much better place to purchase your supplies than your local hardware store.

On the piece in Pictures 48 through 50, I used some black fiber spacers. To lock the black

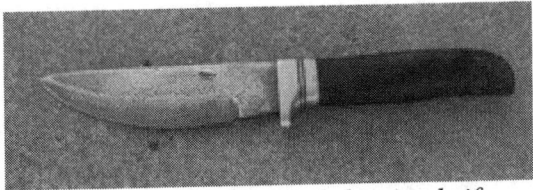

Illustration 50: The finished skinning knife.

material in place, I used a slow setting 50 second cyanoacrolate, commonly called a super glue. The slow setting formula allows plenty of time for me to clamp things before it cures. The normal 3 to 5 second glue sets before I can get everything clamped. If you are not careful and choose the wrong glue, it will swell up the more fibrous spacer materials, which looks bad. I have found using the slow setting cyanoacrylate works well for many different materials.

I mounted the bronze to the blade without the horn, so I could shape the metal without risking heat damaging the horn. After I had gotten the bronze shaped and polished to 400 grit I used 2 part epoxy to attached the horn then carefully shaped the horn to match the contours of bronze. I then finished with the 30 micron belt and hand sanding. When I was test fitting the horn to the tang I decided to add a single black spacer between the bronze fittings and the horn to clean up the transition of that joint.

For regular stock removal knives it takes less than fifteen minutes to profile, drill and grind the blade. After heat treat it can take an hour to assemble the next day. It will take anywhere from 35 minutes to two hours to finish the handle and blade to a mirror polish.

This example was a composite handle of various materials. If you wish you can use only stabilized wood. These are great for handles on kitchen knives and many colors are available.

Two Piece "Sandwich" Handle

Occasionally, you will want a full guard as in the last example. However, because of the material thickness available, you need to use 2 scales rather than a full block to make your handle. Cut a slot in each scale and remember to intentionally leave some extra space in the slot. Because you will be using epoxy, you need enough space for the epoxy. Place the tang in the slot then cut, and mark the scales for the holes. Drill the tang for the 1/8 inch diameter pins you will be using. Cut the pins about an inch long.

When I drill the handles I do one at a time, using the holes in the tang as a guide. Making sure its straight, I use masking tape on the face of the wood to prevent splitting when the drill bit comes through. Mark this and after the first side is drilled out, proceed with the other side.

Now what you have is a tang inside the handle. Remember to include enough excess room for epoxy and everything should be solid. Place the handle materials in place and use 2 inch C clamps to keep it in place while it sets.

You can tell if enough epoxy has been used when you apply the clamps, because the excess comes out from between the scales seams. Let it set up first. The epoxy is much easier to clean up once it hardens.

Trim off this glue, and then knowing it is over-sized, you can remove the outer layer and have fresh material with no glue/epoxy stains to get in the way of the finish. This stabilized wood is self-finishing, meaning the resins that were used leave a nice finish when polished. It is also water tight so you have what looks like the solid wood handle. This blade will tolerate a dish washer.

To finish the handle, do not use a belt that you already used on metal; it will deposit some metal grit into the handle you are working. Using 120 grit is a good belt to start. Most handle material does not need the 40 grit belts. Using 240 and then 400 grit, buff and you have a finished blade, and handle. Your hands will tell you where it is out of alignment or somehow misshapen. Hold it up to the light by the blade and look to see both sides. Look every place and compare sides, top line and bottom.

Take extra care when grinding next to the front piece, so you do not touch the guard with a belt or buffer. I finished the entire handle, but did not touch that front piece so I did not mess the guard up.

It is good to point out that when grinding soft materials with metal spacers along with them, it is easy to get a scallop effect if you are not careful. Epoxy gives up when heated to about 400°F So remember to keep it cool as you finish the handle.

Hidden Pins

Sometimes we want the added support of pins in a handle without them being seen. For this, drill a few pin holes, and solder or braise in pins that barely protrude above the tang. You do not want these to extend through the face of the scale material. You drill the back side of the scales just deep enough to allow the scale to sit flush against the tang. Glue the scales in place as you did with the 2 piece handle example.

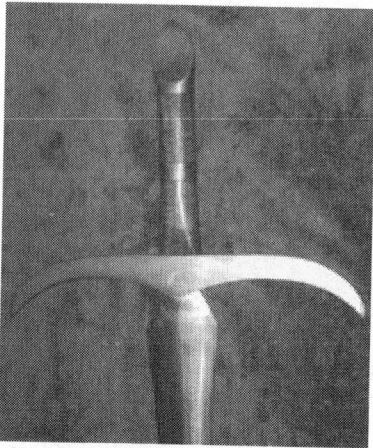

Illustration 51: Sword grip showing split scales and wrought iron hardware.

Here is a different job with the front and rear wood sections of the grip having been cut into 4 sections for installation. Grip is the proper term for the handle of a sword.

I welded the iron spacer and pommel onto the tang first. I then cut an 8 inch long block of figured walnut into equal 4 inch lengths. I cut each of those 4 inch blocks down the middle, using the silver pencil to label each of them so I could identify these sections orientation for alignment when I installed the fit to the tang, glued and hidden pinned the 4 pieces of the wood scales in place.

I actually had to etch the wrought iron after the wood was installed and shaped using Q tips and ferric chloride, masking off the wood areas to protect them from the acid. I had to think of a new way to make the client happy with this sword grip. I did have a few different options requested by the client. As my friend, Glenn Conner likes to say:

"Rather than try to think outside of the box, do not put yourself in a box in the first place".

Frames

I have covered how to cut, fit, punch, slot, and install guards. Another option I need to cover is called a frame, also known as a coffin joint handle. This is used mostly on big knives. If you use a slotted guard, you can use stag or solid wood handle slid over the tang, with or without a butt cap. However you want the guard to go from above the spine and below the ricasso like with a full guard, but want the looks of a full tang I have a solution for you.

A frame lightens the blade, leaving it feeling more like an extension of the hand rather than a block of steel. For this knife I did the guard the same way as the previous blade, but with a small narrow tang.

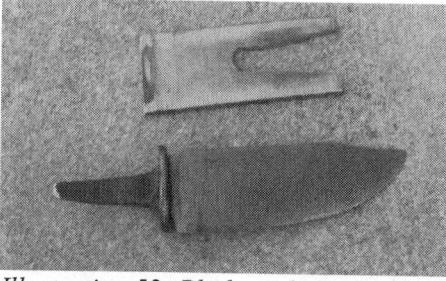
Illustration 52: Blade and tang extension.

I did this so I could slide a guard over it and solder the guard in place. Also because I used pattern welded material, I did not want to waste it on a tang.

In the photo 52 above, the blade is shown with another piece of steel with a "vee" slot cut to match the tang in one end. The slot fits on as shown in this next photo. See how it will come up close to the guard. When I attach this tang extension I can use scales to cover it entirely, treating it the same way as if it were a full tang blade.

I fit the frame piece so that it pushed up tight to the guard and was a nice fit over the tang

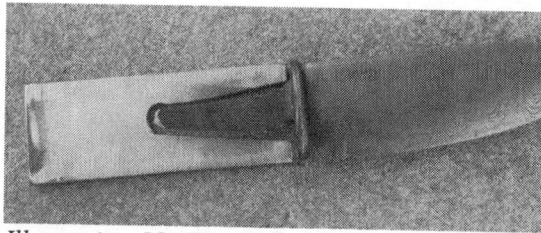
Illustration 53: Test fit.

stub. I left enough guard material on the spine and edge side to trim and finish later. I then silver soldered the handle piece to the tang and solder all of the places around the tang that would show when completed.

Pommels

Some designs want more than just letting the wood or leather handle end, so we add something. This is often a pommel, also called a butt cap.

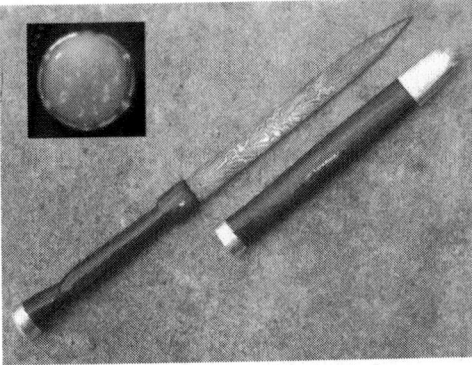
Illustration 54: Scottish style dirk.

The fairly simple method is adding a metal disk to the end of the handle. Here I hard soldered brass into a ring the same size as the finished the wood. I inserted a brass oval sized to fit inside the ring and hard soldered in place. I fit for a carved bone cabochon as well. I had plated this in sterling silver before adding the bone carving but stones or engraving would work as well.

Stone and gems can also be used as spacers, or inset in a pommel as shown by the Scottish dirk in the previous photo. Even wood can have nice end results. Do not be afraid to try new things. If you mess up, remove it and try again, or try another idea. I have made steel mock-ups of handles and blades, to use as a form to hammer the bronze or nickel silver to shape. This is a nice way for form fitting without risking any damage to the blade.

Burning In

Take your handle material, and drill a pilot hole as a guide for the tang. Then heat the tang in the range of a black to a reducing red heat, force the tang along this pre-drilled hole enlarging it to fit using lots of water to avoid ruining the handle itself. Just dunk the handle in water between burnings to prevent it from being damaged. Then heat the tang again and repeat until you have the tang seated. The last one I did took 3 heats to get it set properly in black walnut. After the wood dries, place epoxy on the tang and install the handle for a permanent mount. This can get messy.

Scales

Some materials do not lend themselves to a solid block for handles. Other times you might want the tang to be exposed. Use thin 1/4 to 3/8 inch thick pieces referred to as scales. This allows things like Mother of Pearl or Abalone to be used for handle material. Hollow the center of the tang so that it leaves a little room for glue or epoxy making a stronger joint.

As mentioned earlier, if you are using stag or other material where the surface needs to remain intact, remove excess thickness from the back side of the scale to preserve that face textures and colors. Then drill the scales to match the holes already drilled in tang.

Mark both scales with a Sharpie® then hollow grind them from behind to take away enough material to fit. Make sure the little angle where the edge of the scale meets the bolster is correct, and that the scale is thin enough so the outside does not have to be ground away and lose color.

When using mother of pearl, or other translucent material, try using aluminum foil between the tang and the scale to aid in reflecting light through the material, you will be surprised at how much better it looks. For most things I will use a black paper liner purchased from a hobby shop. I suggest you leave the paper oversize and trim later. I used 1/4 inch mosaic pins on this bowie.

I drill without paper in place, so when I add paper it will make a tight seam of the bolster and scales. Use a piece of leather over the outside surface of the scale. I used six clamps on this knife, though some may have needed more to

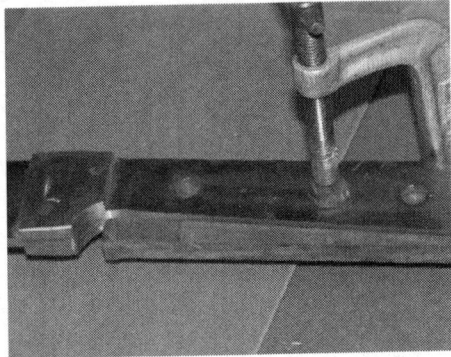
Illustration 55: Setting up.

hold flat and secure. Tighten each clamp a little bit, one at a time. Drill two holes and drop the pins in. The leather will keep the pins off the floor. Dip the end of each pin in white glue before pushing in to help hold them in place. Drill the other two holes. Hold this in your hand and push up into the drill, try and miss your fingers, because bleeding on the scales may stain them. Then take this scale off the tang, and set up the other scale for drilling on the other side.

Eyeball the wood angle a lot while you drill and try to keep straight and square with everything. This is not a Swiss watch but if you take pride on your work, it will show. Then take this second side apart and check alignment by cleaning off any white glue residue and test fitting all of the parts.

Mix your epoxy and smear on the tang before putting on the paper. Put more epoxy on the face of that paper then lay one scale in place. The sharp pins will push through the paper and a little bit out other side of the tang. Flip over and glue that side of the tang, pushing the paper onto the pins, and glue the face of the paper before adding the last scale. This will tell you if all holes line up. You would have checked them many times already so by now there should be no problems.

Epoxy Trick

I get powdered pigment from knife suppliers and dye the epoxy. A little dab helps hide any little imperfection on the wood where it meets spacers. Also, you can grind up whatever materials you are using for handles and add that to the epoxy for filler to blend in better. Feel free to experiment with other colors for matching the materials you choose to use, but be aware that a darker color hides better than a lighter color does. Glue joints will fail if used to fill a void. I prefer to use epoxy, because it is usually stronger than the parts being used.

Chapter 8

Sheath Making

When you make knives someday someone may wish to carry one of them. You can purchase pre-made sheath's for carrying blades from a store, but they will never have a proper fit to your custom blades. A knife sheath is not hard to make. This section covers how to make your own sheaths. Like everything smiths do there are many ways to make a sheath and this covers only a few of those ways.

Making a Leather Sheath

Almost all of the tools I use are available from Tandy Leather®. They have several books that show more detailed information about leather working and also send out free catalogs for finding supplies and tools.

Illustration 56: Tools for making the sheath.

Here is a photo showing some of the tools I use.
Starting from the left:

- Leather wax
- Leather dye
- Rubber mallet
- Dividers
- Hole punch, set and snaps
- Marking pen
- 2 prong hole punch (for curves
- 6 prong punch makes holes for stitching
- Thread, sewing needles
- Scissors
- Slitter
- Groover

I use the alcohol-based dyes on my sheath. Some prefer to use water-based or oil-based. You may have to dye the leather several times until you get the look you like, but two coats has been plenty for me. I put on the coats with a cotton ball and, when the leather is dry, I lightly hand sand it and then apply one more coat to make it smooth and even. I will dye this one after I finish so the photos are clear, but normally it is a good idea to dye the leather first so there are no undyed spots after the sewing.

I use 4 to 5 oz leather for sheaths. The leather cuts better if you wet it first. Lay the knife on the leather and using scissors cut a pieces leaving enough extra around the

Illustration 57: Lay out leather.

blade for the stitching. Several times you will expose the blade to wet leather and if you have a carbon steel blade please take the time to wipe the moisture from your blade to prevent rust.

This picture shows a right handed welt type sheath. Lay out the location for the snaps with the dividers and awl. I use the grooving tool to lay out the line for the stitching. It actually cuts a shallow trench below the surface of the leather for the thread to lay flat.

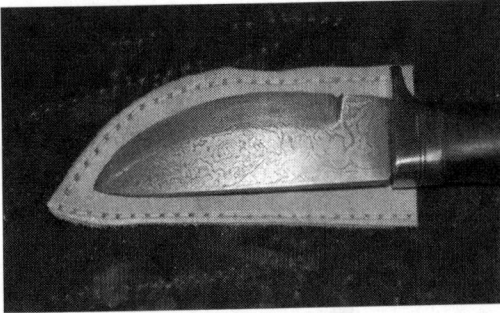

Illustration 58: Trimmed to fit.

Mark up another piece of leather and lay it on the inside of the sheath. Cut this leather piece to match the blade and use it as a spacer, called a billet.

Lay the knife on the billet and mark around where you will cut it to fit. The billet is a key to making the knife fit in the sheath. If you do not plan spacing, when you put a billet in and sew the sheath together the knife edge may cut the threads.

This next picture shows how the billet follows the edge of the blade and leaves room for the guard. The billet will need to be thicker on this sheath to make room for the handle and guard.

Glue two more pieces of leather on top of the billet. You can use rubber cement or barge cement for this to hold things in place for sewing. Use a razor or skiving tool to taper the last two pieces you glued onto the billet. I use the contact wheel on the grinder. The tool has a blade in it; use it to cut the leather thinner. You also can use a sharp knife or razor blade;

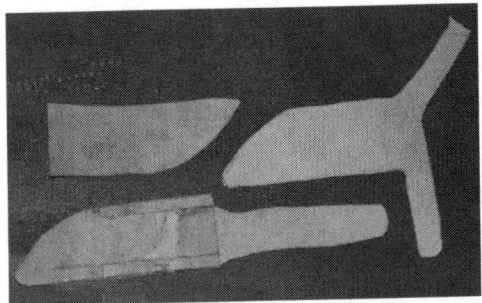

Illustration 59: Billet in place.

I use a 120 grit belt on my grinder to trim the edges. Picture 60 shows the edge of the sheath showing the billets, and how they taper down in thickness to blend into a smooth line along the edge. The sheath is ready to be stitched.

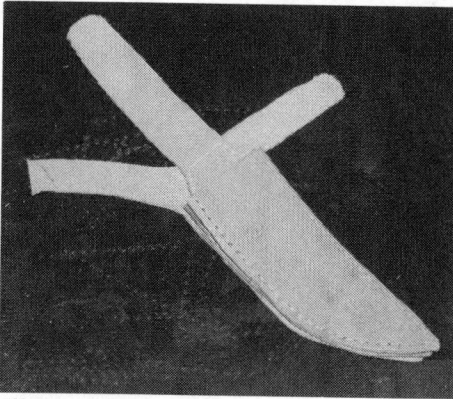

Illustration 60: Ready to sew.

After sewing, wet the whole sheath with water and push the knife in. Using your fingers, or a push stick, mold the sheath around the knife so it has a snug fit. Remove the knife and let the sheath dry. Then I use a belt grinder to dress the edge of the sheath and smooth it up so all pieces of the billet and outer layers appear as one. I use a 120 grit belt for this. You could shave the edge with a blade and hand sand the edge.

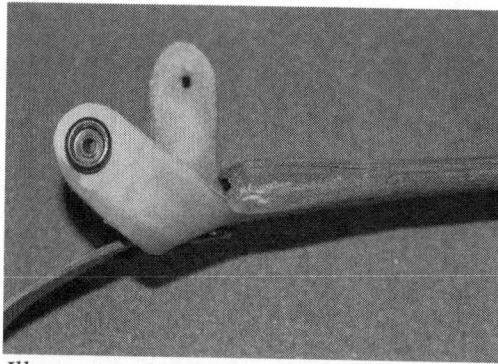

Illustration 61: One snap installed, See the edges of the layers?

Once the sheath is all glued up and in a clamp called a stitching horse, start the first stitch in the second hole and pull about 20" out the other side for this size sheath.

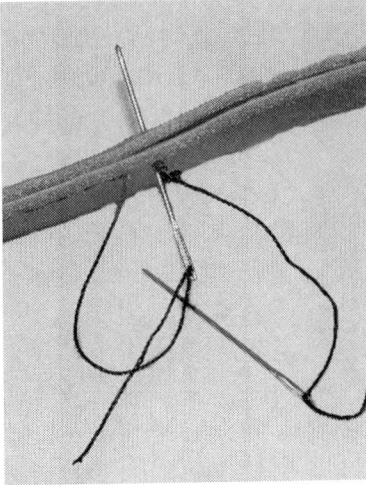

Illustration 62: Dual needles stitching.

Photo 62 shows where I have pulled the threads through. The second needle always goes back through the same hole as the first needle. This is called a saddle stitch.

Stitch the thread into the first hole. Keep the tension the same all through the sewing for a clean look, if you do not, it will pucker and curl from the tension.

When you get to the end of the sheath start stitching back and sew about three or four holes to lock the thread tightly. Knot and pull the ends of the string though a nearby hole to hide it.

Now it is time to put some finishing touches on the seam. Lay the sheath on its face side on something hard and smooth. Tap flat on the back of the seam all down its length with the mallet. Different styles of knives may take different types of sheath's. Picture 63 is the photo of the finished sheath for the skinning knife I made earlier.

Another option is a fold over type. To fit that type of sheath make a billet to go part way around the knife and be sewn in like the other. You would need only one billet on one side.

I hope this gives you an idea on where to begin. It may just let you know your leather work is better than mine. I feel that when I spend a lot of time on a knife it is only right to compliment it with a well-fitting and attractive sheath.

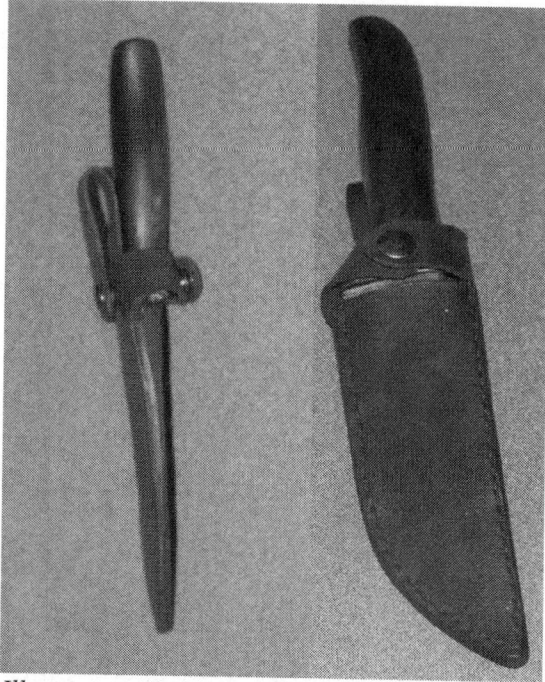

Illustration 63: Here is the dyed and finished sheath we just made.

Wooden Scabbards

This section shows how to make a sheath from wood, with leather lining, using metal hardware. Soft woods are not always the best choice. If the wood will be visible, you want an attractive color and grain pattern. An example of this is making the scabbard for a Viking broad sword. I am using a sword to give me enough space for inserting a liner, but you could use the same general methods for a dirk.

As with the previously mentioned applications, it is best to use stabilized woods. If you are using fiddle back grain or heavy burls, stabilizing is needed to keep it from falling apart over time. By starting with one thick piece and splitting it, you match the grain for later when the scabbard is finished. Two separate boards are not likely to look as one, this method resolves that problem. Mark the inner sides at one end so they align later more easily. After carving and rough sanding the insides with 80 grit, rough shape the outside of the scabbard, leaving no less than a ¼ inch thickness of wood all around the cavity you just carved out.

Now lay the blade on the wood, tracing the outline of the blade, then repeat for the other side. Use a mill or hand held rotary tool to cut about half the thickness of the blade deep into each side. This means that if the sword is 1/4 inch thick at its base, cut both sides 1/8 inch deep. Carefully remove the wood in the areas the blade slides in and hand sand with 80 grit; it is going to be a little large, and that is good, because you will need that extra room to hold the liner.

Test fit the blade until there is easy play when you insert and remove the blade. You can check by coating the blade with colored chalk used for carpenters string lines.

Lining a Scabbard

Now you are ready to insert the light 1 to 2 ounce weight leather liner for the scabbard. This liner will hold protective oils to prevent rusting of the blade over time. Avoid chrome tanned leather for anything that comes in contact with metal because it is corrosive to steel. Use vegetable tanned leathers. Dr. J. Hrisoulas suggests lambs skin is best to use due to its natural lanolin.

The trick to making a leather liner is to open the scabbard and start with one side. Lay in the leather liner. Use simple white school glue to hold the leather in place. The white stuff never lasts like other glues. This temporary hold allows you to check spacing again.

The blade should still slide in and out easily. If not, remove the liner from that side and sand the wood a little more, enlarging the cavity slightly. After the blade fits properly and still sits slightly loose do the same to the other side of the scabbard. Now with both sides having this temporary liner, the blade should still grab a bit after a few test fits. After you get the blade to slightly grab as it slides smoothly all the way in and out again, clean off the white glue and prepare for final mounting of the liner.

I like a blade to sit solidly and not wobble around when at rest in the sheath. You want a little tension between the scabbard and the blade when inserted. Trim off any excess liner. This time reinstall the liner using a more permanent glue. I like to use yellow wood glue because it holds well enough and can be removed if you have to make any repairs later.

After gluing this liner down onto both sides of the scabbard, clamp the sides together again. Use 20 to 30 of the 2 inch C clamps, like you did when you were test fitting the blade. Then place the blade inside the sheath and allow the glue to dry. This step of leaving the blade in place keeps a bubble from forming under the liner which may block the blade's insertion later. Using so many clamps is not because it has to be very tight, but you want the pressure to be very even.

Let this set over night. After it is dry, you can remove all the clamps and check the insides, trimming the rest of each side of any extra leather that hangs over the slotted area. We want a nice meeting of the leather with no overlaps, or extra hanging out the opening of the scabbard.

Up to now, this is still just a rough shaped block of wood with leather liner added. Use a new 80 grit belt to grind out the final outer profiles for your scabbard. Get this very close to what is wanted for a final contour, before starting on making the hardware.

Hardware

A shaped wooden scabbard can be attractive, but to really make it stand out, we embellish the scabbards with hardware. It is not advisable to form hot metals onto wood directly. I made templates from mild steel, shaped like the wooden ends of sword and knife sheaths, to form my fittings for the tip, called the chape, as well as the entrance place called the locket.

Clamp these into a vise and use as swages for forming the metal. You also may use stake anvils. You can work hot or cold. Test fit the hardware to the wood without fear of burning the sheath material because you can let the metals cool before you test fit them to the sheath. Remember as you work hot metal its size will be different than after it cools due to expansion and contraction issues, so do not rush.

The slotted end where the blade enters is the piece of hardware called a locket. Use a simple a ½ inch wide 16 gauge or thinner piece of brass, shape by wrapping it around the form you made, and braise it closed. Add an oblong disk and make the slot for the blade to insert. Glue up the locket and chape and slip them into place. You can add details by engraving or setting stones, however you wish.

Hot Fitting

While I mentioned it is not a good idea to hot fit on wood, one notable exception was a request I had for wrought iron fittings on a scabbard with belt mounting that had secondary fittings about 6 inches away from the locket. I forged them around a mild steel form to rough shape, then I hot fit on the over sized wood of the scabbard near the locket and quenched fast to cool and shrink fit. I used pins to hold this loop tight.

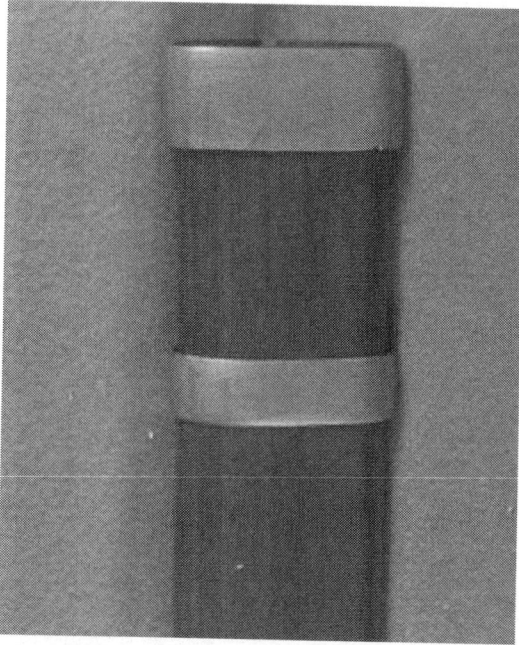

Illustration 64: Iron fittings on a wooden sheath

After cooling, I removed the extra thickness of now partially burnt wood, so no burned wood remained after bringing the scabbard to size. This process works well as long as you remember to plan for the scorching during the fitting process and the need to remove that wood afterward.

There was still the need to etch the wrought iron fittings. To do this, protect the wood with the application of a double coat of varnish, to be removed later, and apply the ferric chloride, alternating with hydrochloric acid to etch and add topography. Q-tips© are handy to apply both acids and the neutralizers. If you are working on small areas you may be able to use just a coating of wax as a resist against the etchant.

When neutralized, remove the heavy coat of varnish along with any stray acids discoloration. After full cleanup do a proper sanding and apply the final finish. When you have worked so hard on a blade, it does not make sense to cut corners on fit, finish or materials.

Chapter 9

Forge Welding

Long before there were arc welders, blacksmiths welded iron in the forge. As a result, smiths discovered that various alloys when layered can look attractive. Do not worry about any fancy patterns yet, as that will be covered later in this chapter. When smithing was a common trade in nearly every city, a new apprentice started learning by cleaning the master's shop, and forge welding the scraps left over from the shops past jobs into one bar for use in the shops future jobs. Forge welding is not an advanced skill but a basic smithing procedure.

Let's start by joining two metals together. The main thing to remember is to clean the steel and to keep the fire clean and not use any more air flow than needed.

No coal supply is perfect. A coal forge can collect clinkers. Clinkers are formed from the burnt residue from the coal we use, which can look like a light gray crunchy lump and sometime even dark glass. Much of the clinker is made of oxidized nonferrous metals and impurities from the steel. Every so often our fire does not seem to be able to get hot enough, that usually is caused by clinkers building up and blocking the air flow.

You need to pull out the burning center of the fire, remove this mass from the coal, return the burning coals back to the fire pot before you can resume your work. This operation does not take long, Not doing it, however, can prevent a good weld because the clinker is blocking the air flow and absorbing heat. For forge welding you need more heat than we do while performing more general forge operations.

In a gas forge you need to have a reducing fire. Just a little flame coming out the entrance, called the dragon's breath, is a good sign of a reducing fire. You do not want an excess of flame exiting the forge because that is wasting your money on excess fuel.

To clean the steel use 40 or 50 grit belts, leaving the scratches across the bar, not along with its length, to assist in the removal of any contaminants when welding. Wire tie them into one unit and heat the steel to a dull red, then lightly coat with the flux. I use about a tablespoon of flux for covering a 1 x 1 inch square bundle, extending about 3 or 4 inches; you do not need much. Return this bundle to the fire and allow the bar to get hotter. Exactly how hot depends on the steels used and your shop. I may call the heat color orange for welding. Others may say cherry red. A few may call it yellow. We all perceive color a bit differently.

If you have never forge welded before, learn to weld by using scrap mild steel. By now you should know how hot mild steel can get in your shop before it starts to burn. For forge welding you want to be just below that point. After you get proficient at that, then begin with the higher carbon steels, which will seem easier, since they weld at much lower temperatures than the mild steel.

Pattern Welding

If you cannot do basic forge welding perfectly, this is a good time to learn how. Pattern welding is a technique I do not recommend for new makers. Pattern welding is where a smith manipulates forge welded layers of steel into controlled patterns. This is an advanced technique, but there is no reason a person can not learn to forge weld different metals into one bar.

Remember to use only gentle taps to start the weld. Some times the weld may barely stick, or only a few layers have welded while others did not. This is nothing to worry about; simply brush off any scale, flux, and repeat the process.

After the bar is solidly made into one piece then you can hit it harder. Also note that rebar is not good to use when learning, either. It is junk to start with, because it is not consistent. You will never know what was your mistake and what was caused by the junk in the rebar.

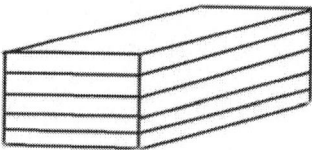

After all it was made to strengthen concrete and nothing else.

After you gain those skills take a rather simple billet, such as 6 layers of 1084 and 5 layers of 15N20 steel bar stock. This combination makes a nice contrast and both of these steel types will make a nice knife on their own.

Carbon Migration

There are no high and low carbon content layers to pattern welded steels. Some layers may be softer in the end but that is only due to the nature of that layers alloys. Not all elements migrate as fast as carbon does. According to metallurgist Thomas Nizolek:

When we forge weld steels together, the carbon content in any layer of steel will equalize with that of the surrounding layers of steel very quickly. In Pennsylvanian, February 2009, Laboratory testing was made on a forge welded billet made from 4 alternating bars of W2 and 203E. This examination was done with an electron microscope. In the four layer sample it is evident, based on the pearlite gradient between the layers, that extensive carbon diffusion occurred after the first weld course. Drawn out and folded, the eight-layer sample showed that the pearlite concentration has almost equalized, however ferrite still decorates the prior-austenitic grain boundaries in the 203E layer. By the time the material has reached 16 layers, the carbon content of the sample appears to be uniform. (1)

1 - Jacquet-Lucas Award:
Metallography of a Modern Pattern-Welded Steel Knife Blade, Thomas Nizolek, Advanced Materials & Processes, *Volume 167, Issue 2, February 2009*

This appears to prove that carbon migration is happening much faster than most smiths had thought in years past. This means that the patterns we have in a billet made from using only simple carbon steels, must be coming from the other alloy differences, and not from the carbon as we use to think.

Getting a usable blade means paying attention to our steel's alloy content, which includes the amount of carbon. If the carbon content is too low it will not harden. So a 1095 and 1005 mix will not result in a very hard blade, partially due to carbon migration, because using equal parts of 1095 and 1005 will result in the equivalent of about 1045 in the finished billet.

The simple math says 0.50 carbon, but remember to account for the loss of carbon to the atmosphere during welding, as well.

Carbon has a stronger attraction to air than to steel. This condition will also cause some of the carbon from the surface layers of our blade to move into the atmosphere. This is another reason to leave the blade thick before hardening. It allows us enough extra material to still have plenty of thickness left after our final grinding, which removes this de-carb layer as we remove the scaling caused by the quenchant.

Building a Pattern

If you take a layer of high carbon steel, such as the 1084 and a layer of mild steel, and weld them together, the carbon migrates from the areas of higher concentration into the lower, and the carbon will equal out. You must be aware of that when we make a billet that will be made into a knife.

For this example I will be using 1084 and 15N20. The dark is the 1084. The 15N20 has nickel in it and is the bright layer. This is the start of a basic billet. The process produced a 1 inch x 1 inch x 12 inch long billet after the first weld.

Draw out this billet to about 3/4 inch square and cut it into four pieces. I combine and assemble them as in the following illustration. To forge weld this together, you have to grind clean every surface that will weld before you can tack one end together and use wire to keep the bars in position.

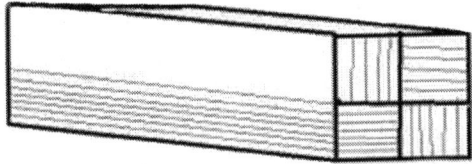

Here I have wrapped the 4 bars with another pattern to make a nice hammer. Look at that pattern and think about how it would look if you drew it out and got four more bars from it. They would be small, but you could weld them just like you did before. Another idea would be to cut across the piece on an angle to make even more complex patterns. You could make a jig to hold the billet so you can easily cut this billet on the diagonal with a band saw. If you forge those shapes the pattern will

Illustration 65: Pattern welded hammer.

change a lot. Think about what would happen with any of these patterns if you just twisted it up tight then flattened them or cut into them like you would do when making a ladder pattern.

Or you could cut across the piece leaving each piece a half inch thick and get what is called tiles. You could weld them side to side and make a long piece of the same repeated pattern. If this was again welded together side by side, you would be building a grid like pattern. All these possibilities could come from the four bars you had when you began. Remember this could be made into something other than a knife, such as a bowl or a chess board.

Can Welding

Sometimes you want to weld up tiles, stainless steel, or even odd shaped pieces and powdered steel into a billet, making what smiths call a mosaic. You cannot always weld these by wiring them as before, but you can easily weld them inside a box like enclosure, a method many smiths refer to as a can weld.

To can weld, make a box from square pipe, welding the ends closed with the bars inside. Alternatively make the can using mild steel (1/8" plate will work - and completely enclose the billet). This contains our materials and excludes air. Place a single layer of newspaper inside the box, and load the box with the bars, tiles, odd shaped pieces, and/or powders. The paper will burn up and remove any oxygen that remains inside so it does not need flux. Drill a small 1/16 inch hole in each end of the can to allow pressure to escape and prevent the can from exploding. Forge the can with its contents into a solid. Afterwards the can will peal away from the billet inside as I grind the surfaces clean.

No matter what pattern you choose, remember that every mating surface of a billet needs to be ground clean first.

The welding shops sell a non-stick spray for welding. Spray the inside pieces of the mild steel you are using to

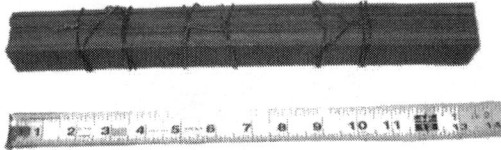

Illustration 66: Cleaned billet wired together.

make the can, then place the billet parts inside and weld it up. After you forge this into a solid block, the mild can will separate cleanly when you grind. Then lay three tiles side by side.

Tack the tiles on the sides where they touch so they will stick together. Weld them together solidly by tapping on the ends of the assembly. Now you are just doing two welds, and have three tiles together. You could twist it and lay it along those tiles and forge weld it again. If you wish, weld a square piece of 1095 alongside of the 3-tile billet you just made for a cutting edge. The possibilities are endless.

I am blending two fairly different processes to make new and unusual patterns - can welding and the billet welding that is done outside of cans. I will use kerosene rather than paper in this can.

For billets without a can, I am very traditional in my ways. I grind each and every mating surface and wire the stack every few inches. I always use a flux.

I know of some smiths that like to arc weld the billet together, but I feel this can contaminate the final billet with the weldment, and I prefer to avoid it. When a bar in the billet expands it can shift position when I use wire to hold it in position. If I had arc welded that same billet in place, it could not shift, so it warps and buckles, leaving a gap that is hard to close up.

When initially arranging the mixed materials in the stack, I have the higher heat tolerant items placed at the outside of the stack to protect the inner layers so there is a lesser a risk of burning them. Remember to always watch the temperatures.

When heating, be sure to have the layers of the billet vertical, to allow the heat to transfer completely through the stack easier. This is more important in a coal forge than in a gas forge because of the directional heating in the coal forge.

Place the billet in a gas forge that is preheated and turned off. This preheats the billet all the way to the center to avoid shocking the steel, which can cause cracking.

After the steel starts to glow a dull red, fire up the forge and flux the piece. If the flux does not stick, warm the billet a bit more until it does. Do not allow the piece to come to a temperature that allows scale to form before fluxing. When you make the first weld you have a lot of time to prepare the piece. You do not want to have problems in a welded billet.

When drawing the billet out, remove every piece of scale from every side to be welded, and repeat the steps above. Wire brush the sides and reflux before each and every heat. Only forge at a welding heat.

I only use new steel for my billets, and what I do is working well for me. Borax stops oxygen from getting to the metal and forming scale where the layers meet. Use what you wish. Some smiths have used a light coating of WD40®, and many other things can work also. WD40® will burn up before the borax melts, leaving the steel clean, while protecting it at the lower temperatures in the forge. When the billet has approached welding heat, the borax takes over.

The atmosphere inside a can is not the same as that to which the billet gets exposed in an open forge. Kerosene, paper, WD-40® or other things are used to remove all of the oxygen inside the container and prevent the scale.

I cringe when I hear someone tell me "it was in an internet video." We do not know the qualifications of the person in the internet video, nor can we see the final results being used. We have to sort out the validity of these for ourselves.

I strongly recommend the series of books by Dr. Jim Hrisoulas for every blade shop. You can also learn a lot from his videos on making pattern welded blades. Never forget that more is learned in your shop than at a computer keyboard. Feel free to use the internet to ask questions, but to get anywhere, you must do it in your shop.

Patterning the Billet

Some of the more basic and long lasting patterns are not out of reach of most of you. I mentioned the ladder pattern. To get this effect, build up your billet to about 70 or more layers. Leaving it about a 3/8 to a half inch thick, cut notches on both sides, to about 1/3 of the way through, making sure the cuts alternate from side to side. At welding heat flatten the billet to expose the ladder effect, which is caused by the layers from the bottom of the cut being brought to the surface of the billet.

Illustration 67: Ladder.

Do not allow the cuts to be directly back to back. There are variations making use of this cutting technique. An example is shown in photo 69; this is what I call my zebra pattern. This is cut like a ladder pattern as well. For this pattern, make 3 billets of 50

Illustration 68: Cuts that create the ladder pattern.

to 100 layers. After squaring them, twist two of the bars one direction and the third the opposing way. Stack them on top of each other with the odd direction twist in the center and weld them, not side by side, but one on top of the other. Flatten out the billet a bit and cut like the normal ladder pattern; however, you need to cut almost half way through into the center of the bars twists.

If you lay the bars side by side, using 5 bars or more, and do not make any cuts, you get the Persian Ribbon pattern shown in

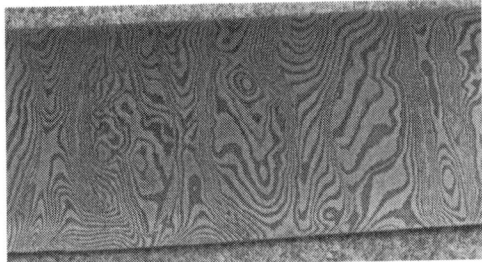

Illustration 69: Zebra

photo 70. One major change with this example of the Persian is the use of three metals rather than only two.

Illustration 70: Persian.

This blade used 1084, L6, and salvaged wrought iron to give more color in the final blade. But you can use only two steels if you prefer.

Do not be afraid of combining various other billet designs into one. The Vikings were doing this over 1,500 years ago. In Picture 71, the center core is a 7-layer billet on its edge that was cut like a ladder pattern and flattened, to be used edge up. On each side of that bar was add a twisted bar to each side, then the last bar was made of a 600-layer laminate to give the cutting edge.

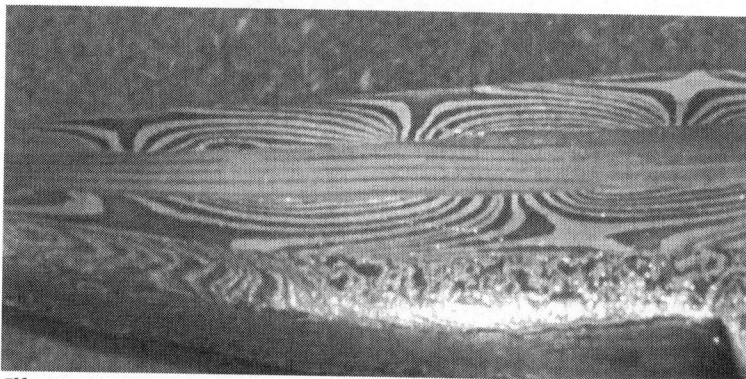

Illustration 71: Multi core.

Use colored modeling clay to experiment with new pattern ideas without risking any steel being ruined. This lets you see how the layers being manipulated look when flattened into a blade thickness. Surface patterns will be different if left thick than if ground into the billet to expose the inner layers. A star pattern is a simple twist, ground down to thickness exposing what looks like stars from the twisted inner layers being brought to the surface. If you forge to profile or choose to grind in the bevels, each option will affect the final appearance of the pattern.

The amount of twisting and forging will change the end result. A high layer count with a loose uneven twist forged to shape gives a maidens hair pattern.

Rather than hope to get nice looks in a basic random pattern, drill shallow holes of various diameters in the billet before each session of the drawing out and welding course to get this pool and eye pattern.

I have showed you how to make repeatable patterns in a combination of ways. We looked at welding tiles together in repeatable patterns.

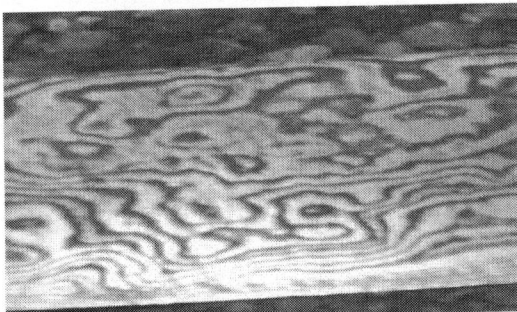
Illustration 72: Pool & eye.

Think about how to reverse engineer other patterns to make them for yourself. You can take apart any of the patterns by eye and see not only where they weld together but also how each pattern is made. I want you to be able to do more than only what I am showing you. I want you to use your imagination to come up with things on your own as well.

Early Origins

Early steel production in many cultures was produced from black sand, bog iron, or local ores that were heated for a long time at near-melting temperatures to separate the iron from the impurities. The result of these early furnaces is called a bloom.

A bloom is a large spongy mass full of slag of mainly silicon, that needed to be folded, or forge welded many times to remove the impurities, resulting in wrought iron, which is normally very low in carbon. After being placed in a box and packed in carbon, it would be heated for a week or more. The reaction is known as carbonizing and results in blister steel. The blister steel would be stacked into a faggot and welded up into what is called *shear steel*.

The original Damascus was a crucible steel. While it was also produced by the use of long times at high heat, this process actually allowed the metal to become molten during its refinement. Known by various names such as Wootz, or medieval Damascus, or even Bullat, these steels have the patterning formed by what is called alloy banding. It has little if anything in common with the pattern welding that I just described.

The Vikings made some of the most marvelous broad swords ever seen, as found at the burial mount of Sutton Hoo, England. Some of the blades found had 9 pattern welded cores with an outer cutting edge steeled into place. Many had jewel encrusted guards and pommels.

The Japanese sword smiths started out with a type of steel of about 1.5 to 2% carbon, made from the black sands of Fe_3O_4 but after driving off the O_2 and repeated folding, they would finish up with a carbon content of around 0.6% to their blades due to loss of carbon in the fire during the folding and refining process.

Forget about making a super sword of 1,000,000 layers. Not only is it impractical to waste that much labor, metal and fuel to try to get there, but if we did continue to re-weld that many times, we still would not have that many layers. After the layers are reduced to the thickness of an atom, they cannot get any thinner; the metal only gets displaced.

Today

If you are not up to this level of highly skilled work, then put in the time and effort with the basics for now, and eventually you will get there. While it may be hard to believe, this level of skill is not beyond the reach of anyone willing to put in the effort.

Now that good steels are readily available nearly everywhere, the practice is used for aesthetics. In all cases today the pattern welded blades are for looks; they are no stronger or better than modern mono steels, and unless one first masters forge welding 100%, the pattern welded blade will be weak and less than a good blade should be.

Every time we do a "fold" or stacking for a forge weld, we lose 5% or more to scale from our billet, reducing the amount of steel we started with. We are also losing carbon content to the atmosphere. Even 30 folds of 1095 has reduced the carbon content to an amount close to that of mild steel and will not make a good blade or hold an edge.

Welding the billet does take effort, but it is not as slow to get a nice pattern as some may think. When only two layers get welded together, and we make one fold onto itself, it results in four layers, the next fold results in eight layers because we continue to double the count with each weld. After only 10 folds we have 1024 layers in the billet which is too fine for most people to see.

Common sense tells me there are faster and better ways to get our layer count up. Starting with seven layers, you can get this layer count up even faster. The next weld would give 14 if you folded in half. I prefer to cut the billet into 3 and stack and weld resulting in 21 layers after the first "fold," and 63 for the next, then 189 and so on. With the same amount of labor to weld, and about the same fuel an 2 layers, you reduced the total scale loss to time being in the forge at heat. Not all steels work together easily. Some pull apart when cooling due to differing expansion and contractions rates. If you are just starting out please review this chapter a few times, and practice on mild steel scraps. This process is for people who already have some experience blade smithing, and want more advanced techniques to practice. I advise learning to forge weld before trying the pattern welding as many patterns place a lot of stress on the weld and, if not 100% solid, will pull apart.

Many factors are involved in getting a solid bond. One of these factors is our drawing out the billet which stretches the weld surface area allowing non-contaminated fresh material to move across the weld boundary. This breaks up any surface imperfections that may interfere with the weld. Do not overlook the importance of the grains reforming across the weld zone as a result of thermal cycling.

Selecting Materials for Pattern Welding

Be aware that carbon is not usually picked up fast enough in a forge to offset what is lost to the atmosphere. The fire does not add any carbon content to the billet. In fact, by the end of your welding and forging session, the total amount of carbon in the billet is a bit less than the total was when you first began, because some carbon is always leaving the steel as carbon, bonding with the oxygen in the atmosphere of the forge at the high temperatures at which we are working, making **CO**. Carbon is further oxidized to **CO$_2$** that goes right up our flues.

Luckily for us today there are many great steels available ready to use. We have a lot less hassle than our forefathers experienced. One key to remember about pattern welded steel, is that it is only as good as the person forge welding it. Bad forge welds will result in a bad billet, no matter what steels were used.

I prefer to use only steels that make good blades by themselves. To limit this problem caused by carbon migration, I suggest starting with 1084 or 1095 and, for the shiny layers, 15N20. Chemically speaking 15N20 is like 1075 with 2% nickel added. These two steels heat and expand at about the same rates. Welding temperatures are very close, and the nickel does not effect it much.

When welding up billets without the covering of a can, we can see the heat creeping up the billet by it changing the color of the steel. If you pay attention you may notice some layers are not exactly the same color as their neighboring layers. This is a sure sign of an incomplete weld that needs your attention. When the weld is good the steel transfers the heat evenly between the layers and there is no separation of the heat colors.

Keep it Simple

If at all possible, work with simpler steels to start like you did when first learning blade work itself. Limit the possible problems you will encounter. Add in more challenges as you learn to use what you have. Jumping all over with various mixes all the time is confusing for pattern welding just as it is with basic forging. You need to allow a little time and experience to gain the skills with one combination before changing your mix of steels.

I do not want to stop anyone from enjoying themselves. I do want you to learn at a pace that is still challenging and rewarding without discouraging you, the new bladesmith, from pushing your limits. I have seen people give up in frustration. I want to eliminate the frustration you may feel from overload.

I heard from a smith that started by using a blade design from a video game with a high alloy steel. After forging he gave it a differential quenching in ice water.

This attempt created all sorts of problems for this over confident smith, including the following:

- Warping
- Twisting
- Cracking
- No hamon

He could not understand what went wrong. Because of adding too many new variables at the same time, he had no way of knowing which new addition caused the problems. This smith gave up. If you slow down and only add one new variable to your training schedule at a time, you can focus on that one new addition.

Pure Nickel

Not all layers of a billet have to be steel that can be hardened. There are occasions where we want to use other things for effect. As mentioned earlier, 15N20 has a low percent of nickel which provides great contrast to a high carbon steel like 1095. Nickel offers nothing but looks to a blade. You heat treat a nickel layered billet the same as you do for the carbon steel used, which in this case is 1095.

I had a sheet of 0.03 inch thickness nickel I cut into one inch wide strips. I layered this with 1/8 inch thick 1095 steel. I did not use any flux at all in this weld, and the surface had to be really clean or it would come apart. I cleaned it with a soak in vinegar. If I had ground it on both sides, there would not be much left so I used a Scotchbrite® pad to clean it.

I use very thin sheets of pure nickel, because nickel tends to alloy with the surrounding steels and appear thicker. You need to be careful about folding too much because of this. There is no carbon migration through pure nickel. The two technically do not weld together, but they do bond well.

The completion of a first weld with this mix would produce an 11 layer billet. Draw the billet three times its 12 inch starting length, then stack and forge weld again; it would be 33 layers. Draw, cut in thirds, and re-stack again for 99 layers, and so on.

Welding Nickel

The way each of these metals expands and the thinness of them prevents you from tacking one end of the stack together, or to wire the billet in in several places and forge weld into one solid block. So I do the first weld as a can weld, starting with a 'U' shaped channel that I made by cutting off one side of a one inch square pipe.

Illustration 73: Loading the can.

You must know the layers orientation inside the can, because you cannot weld them if you are hitting them on their sides. Weld the handle on with a flat edge to show the orientation of the layers. You want to forge this with the edges flat so the flats bond and get thinner. The first heat takes a while to get to welding heat. It has to be hot all the way through, though it will weld at less heat in a can than outside.

When you reduce the thickness by about a third the billet should be one solid block inside. It will all look the same color when solid. You have no further need of the mild steel can. It may still have bonded with the inner billet, but it can all be ground off easily if it does thanks to the newspaper you used.

Non-hardened steel will not look the same before as after the heat treatment. The colors appear a bit washed out until after the blades are hardened.

When you cut and stack and re-weld you will have three pieces, each of which has steel on the outside. You do not need to make a can for this; you wire a couple of places and weld using the flux as before. Pattern this billet however you wish. Nickel delaminates easily when twisted too tight; keeping the billet at welding heat while twisting can help reduce this.

When using multiple billets of twisted bars with pure nickel, you must shim between the billets with carbon steel because the nickel cannot touch itself or there will be a void ruining your work. Nickel will not bond to itself.

One cool thing about using pure nickel sheets is I can use a process from the gun industry known as "hot bluing" for a wild effect. Pure nickel will not take the bluing, which is a controlled rust. But the steel will be a rich dark blue/black; that does not rub off but retains the same level of polish it had before the process.

I have explained how the carbon migrates in a billet. Carbon will not migrate at all through the nickel in this one. So everything not touching the inside of the can will remain at the same carbon content as it was when you started in this bar.

If the billet did weld to the can, at that point of contact you will have carbon migration from the billet into the can. Since there is now proof that carbon fully equalizes after two sessions, it is worth the effort to prevent this, and keep this a high carbon blade.

Cable Damascus

Many smiths have been making a form of damascus from large cables. These end up having a snake skin effect to the pattern of the finished product. It is not a strong pattern, because the color difference is from the decarb zone at the weld lines, not from alloys.

I use 1.5 and 2 inch diameter cables from cranes and dredge lines. Many of these cables are higher carbon. I would guess its possibly AISI 1080 grade. Make sure the cable does not have a fiber core.

Cables are normally covered in a protective coating that must be removed before we can use it. To clean I place the cable in a bucket and cover with kerosene. I have no idea the minimum time needed but I normally allow it to soak for about a week. After removing from the soak, I wire brush and allow to air dry. This removes much of the asphalt and oils used to protect the cables in use.

I have heard of some cables not getting clean enough this way. Then we resort to the long process of unwrapping the wires, after which we can brush them clean, and re assemble. If you have to go to this length of effort, I suggest adding a few thin nickel wires in the wrap for color. Remember that nickel

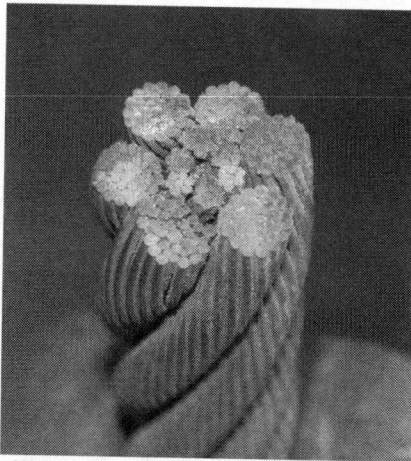

Illustration 74: Cleaned cable before welding.

will not weld to itself, so keep the nickel wires away from each other in the wrap to avoid trouble later.

After getting the cable clean, start by sealing the ends as in the photo above. I have had good success forge welding the ends closed, but I suggest you either MIG or Arc weld the ends together to avoid the cable

unraveling in the forge. Treat this the same way as a normal high carbon bar of steel. Remember to use plenty of flux. To weld the cable into a billet, start with getting the cable to welding heat, then twisting in the vise to tighten up the cable.

Illustration 75: End ARC welded.

After each heat in the fire, alternate between a round of hammering on the cable and twisting on the next heat to tighten up the cable.

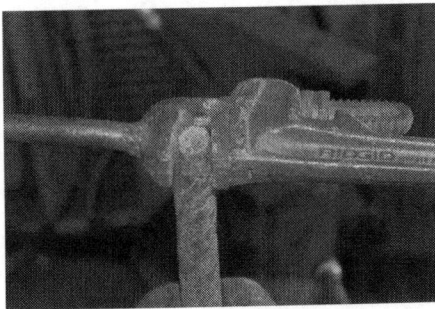

Illustration 76: Twisting wrench.

This continues until you reach the end of the cable. Notice in Picture 76 I added an extra handle to my pipe wrench. This helps keep the billet straight, as well as giving better leverage as I twist. I use this wrench for all my other twisting as well. After twisting, return the cable to the fire to bring it back up to welding heat and weld that same area closed using your swege block. If you do not have a "Vee swege" you can make a simple one with angle iron like in Picture 77. I used 3-inch angle iron to make the "V" part and arc welded on some 2 inch angles for supports. An added piece on the bottom allows this to be held in the hardy hole of my anvil or in a vise.

Illustration 77: Homemade swege.

As the cable welds, its diameter will get smaller and will still fit well in a swege.

Illustration 78: After primary welding.

When you start to forge weld this cable into a solid, it will feel mushy. As the voids start to close up will begin to feel more solid. The advantage of using the swege rather than the anvil face, is that a flat anvil will try to flatten the cable.

As I hammer this cable, I rotate it a quarter turn after each hammer blow. I want to keep this in a round shape for the entire welding course to work the voids from many angles, and the swege helps in this along with the rotation.

At this point it should feel solid, but really it is not. Look at Picture 79. I cut the cable open to show the gaps still remaining after one welding course. There was a lot of empty space within a cable because it is

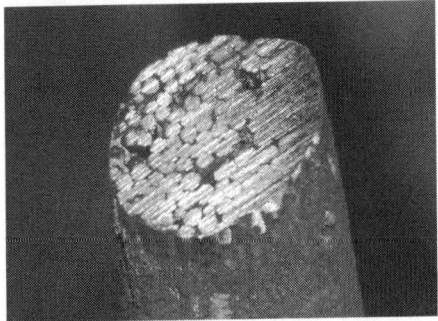

Illustration 79: Inside of cable to show gaps after first weld.

made up of many small round strands. You must close these spaces in order to have a good bar of steel to make our blade. I hope this will help you understand why it is always good to repeat a welding course, even when using flat stock, to make sure your welds are solid.

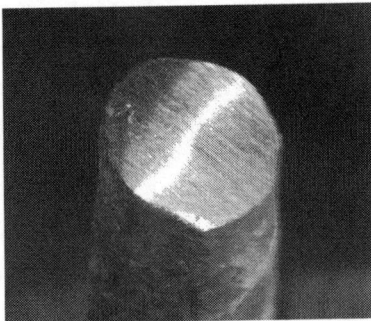

Illustration 80: After second welding course.

After a second welding course most of those voids should have closed up and now you can work this round billet into a flat bar using your anvil. I prefer to keep working this at a welding heat to ensure the voids are getting closed.

After the blade is made, many times you will still have a few pin holes. This seems to be a normal problem working with cables. I may not have figured out the way to eliminate them but I do my best to remove as many as I possibly can.

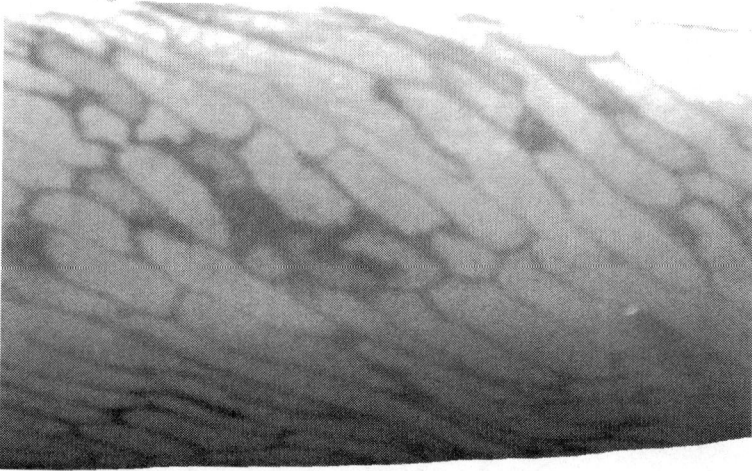

Illustration 81: Finished and etched cable damascus.

Why Flux

When you heat steel hot enough it starts to oxidize. Oxidation creates scale, which can look terrible in a weld, and in many cases, can prevent a good weld. In an attempt to reduce this problem, we must monitor air input to the fire. A reducing fire will leave less air for the formation of any oxides. Scale melts at a much higher temperature than steel. This means if you have scale in the joint, you cannot get a good weld. If there is scale it will show as a black line that likes to rust. If you have it, the only way to fix it is to grind that out and try welding it closed again.

Welding Flux Types

Flux is used to protect the steel from oxygen, which
helps to prevent scale. It also is a corrosive, and as
such cleans the weld joint for you to get a nicer weld.
A side effect of some types of flux is that they dissolve
some of the surface oxides of the steel. As you close
the weld seam it removes contamination from the weld
zone as it is squeezed out. All of this works in favor of
getting a good weld.

Sand

Not all sand is created equal. Where I grew up on lake
Michigan the sand was white silica sand, which is used
for glass making and for flux. Here in Indiana,
however, the sand is full of red clay, which does not
work well as a flux. The silica in the sand melts,
coating the steel to prevent oxidation. Using sand will
not lower the welding temperature of the steel. You
can buy the correct sand from dealers that sell brick
and block.

I am not sure how well sand works when using modern
high alloy steels that burn at higher temperatures. Try
a test piece before you decide to flux on an expensive
billet with your sand.

Wasp Nests/Mud Daubers

Some people use Mud Dauber wasp nests. Grind up the
dried nests and sieve out any bug parts. Use the fine
powders as a flux. This does not lower the welding

temperature. I have been told it is the sand from the mud the wasps used in building these nests that make an effective flux. Be sure to remove any leftover occupants before grinding the nests.

Straw Ash

The Japanese smiths are known to have used burnt rice straw for a flux with their Tamahagane steels for hundreds of years. The ash is mixed with water to form a paste, and when applied to the hot steel coats and protects the steel from oxidation. Many feel this adds a prism type of sheen to the weld line increasing the beauty of the finished steel. Other forms of ash have been effectively used as a flux also.

Kerosene/WD-40®

A few smiths report they are having great results using kerosene or light oils such as WD-40® as the only protection for the steel. It does not seem to affect the welding temperatures, but it does clean the steel and prevents oxidation at lower temperatures, and, in a reducing gas forge seems to work well for many, avoiding any risk of contamination from use of another type of flux.

Commercial Products

There are fluxes that may be purchased from black smith and welding shops to use in forge welding. Some of these commercial products are wonderful.

Some of these commercial mixes have iron filings or other foreign matter included, that while assisting in a good solid forge weld, may leave behind inclusions. These inclusions are not usually a problem in general smithing, but may be seen in a finished blade. Anhydrous borax is used as a base in many of the prepared fluxes.

Borax

Borax is a mineral mined as a relative pure form. A commercially available product called 20 Mule Team® borax can be found at local grocery stores for about $4 for a two pound box, so it is not expensive to purchase.

At room temperature it is used as a mild washing aid. At forge welding temperatures it becomes liquid and coats the steel to prevent oxidation. When heated to liquid, borax has a PH of about 2.2 and is effective in cleaning the steel by dissolving scale. This is extremely corrosive, so take precautions from splatter. It is not only the scale you have to worry about, melted borax will stick to your skin like honey and will not come off until after it cools. Use vinegar to neutralize the corrosive effect and to cool.

The borax available in the grocery store has water chemically bound up in it. Many smiths prefer to cook this water off prior to using it as a welding flux, to prevent the bubbling when put on a hot billet. I do not bother with this extra work, but if you feel it works better for you, then cook off the water. Borax lowers welding temperatures, and I use borax for most all welds. Having said that, borax will not produce good welds with some alloys.

Chrome Oxides

High chrome steels need more than plain borax to weld properly. Many high chrome steels can be forge welded in a coal forge. I have done it and know others that have forge welded AISI D2 as well as true stainless steels.

However not all chrome is freely available to form corrosion resisting oxides because some is molecularly bound up in carbides. Alloy D2 has 12% chrome, but it is not classified as a stainless, the key here is "free chrome."

Typically stainless steels are a family of steels having over 10.5% free chrome in the alloy. The point is that stainless steels properties come from the resistance to corrosion caused by forming a microscopic layer of chrome oxides that protect the steel. This layer can regenerate to near 100 % of its maximum possible thickness within only 15 minutes after grinding. That same chrome layer can form on any steel alloy that includes chrome to a point, and this can effect welding. Many use a mix of about 5% Sal Ammoniac and 95% borax for most alloys such as L-6 and 5160. Sal Ammoniac is a common plumbers flux also known as ammonium chloride. It becomes liquid at a much lower temperature than borax melts, so begins doing its protective work sooner than borax alone.

You may need to add other things to your flux as well for welding stainless steels. Fluorspar is something that is not common to use because it is **very toxic**. If you are going to use fluorspar or any fluorine compound wear a properly rated respirator for working with this chemical. It is especially dangerous to use this additive in the flux without one. **Do not** use this chemical unless you have been trained in its HazMat safety rules and nothing else seems to work. It is dangerous but will clean the chrome oxides to allow a clean forge weld. Most of the flux compounds required for Stainless Steel welding can instantly cause irreparable damage to your lungs as well as other airway tissues, so be aware of bystanders in the area, as well.

Remember this text reaches a lot of people that may not have access to necessary protection from these hazards. Even the borax has some hazards. Please be safe.

In alloys like AISI 52100 and other lower chrome bearing alloys the addition of Boric acid can help a little. If you clean the surface well before the weld, the addition of sal ammoniac and boric acid should be enough to get that to weld for you.

An easy source for getting Boric Acid is to buy a can of Roach Proof® powder. Read the label, and you will find it is 98% boric acid; the remaining 2% is not going to cause a problem for welding.

Summary on Fluxes

A lot of people weld simple steels without flux, and that is fine. But I still recommend that, while starting to learn, use it to make your job easier. After you get good at forge welding, feel free to try new things. I doubt high chrome steels can be forge welded without flux in an open coal forge but I have been wrong before. Stainless steel is another steel choice that

would benefit by using the can weld method.
All of these can work, but not all are easy to use.
Borax is common in many places, and works well.
There are also commercial fluxes available, and some
of them are great, while others are no good for pattern
welding. The addition of iron filings in some
commercial fluxes will leave strange things in the
visible weld lines and that can ruin the looks of your
blade. Whether you wish to try these is up to you.

But I am attempting to get you started. After the start I
do expect people to experiment and learn new things.
I do not have all the answers, only some of the answers
to some questions I have asked myself. In some cases
there are answers I am still seeking myself.

Differential Etching

The pattern at the end of forging and polishing a blade
is most times highlighted by an acid etch. The simple
steels are more reactive to the etching process,
resulting in a darker layer, and nickel and chrome
bearing alloys are brighter because those alloys are
resistant and slower to react to the etchant, resulting in
the differential etching that shows the layering and
patterns we all love in our blades.

Once you have your pattern welded blade polished to
600 grit, or finer, you want to clean it with a window
cleaner or acetone to remove all finger oils, etc, so you
can etch the blade. Use ferric chloride (PC board
etchant , available from most electronics stores) diluted
to 1.5 % strength, or hydrochloric acid (muriatic or
pool acid) acid diluted to 15%. You will get a darker
contrast of colors with the ferric chloride. Muriatic

acid will give a heavier, more pronounced topography. Check the blade every 15 minutes or so to see how the etch is coming along. With a clean paper towel, rub off the black film that develop as it etches to expose more metal to the acids. It should take anywhere from 15 to 45 minutes to get the blade properly etched. Do this at room temperature. It will etch faster if heated, but a slow etch seems to be more even and I have noticed that, no matter how pressed for time I am, there is always time to do it again if the result is poor. A spotty etch looks terrible and the only way to repair that is to re-grind, starting over again.

Occasionally I will use white vinegar for a very slow etch. It does not always get as dark as ferric chloride, but vinegar works nicely for many fine layered patterns, and occasionally brings more than just a light and dark coloration to the finished blade.

There are times when I use multiple etches. Start with a muriatic acid to increase the topographical difference, followed by a light buff and a shorter soak in ferric chloride or vinegar for adding color. Experiment and see what you prefer.

In the next chapter, I will discuss some techniques that go beyond the basics of knife making.

Chapter 10

Beyond Basics

Meteorites

After a time you may wish to work some Meteorites into a usable form, as our forefathers did. This section addresses working with extraterrestrial materials.

Of the 4 major types of metallic meteorites, Octahedrites are of the most concern to us. When properly etched these types exhibit the well-known Widmanstatten pattern. The contents of these meteorites range from about 7% to 12% nickel plus a combined total of 1% cobalt, iridium, and gallium; the remaining is almost pure Iron. Meteorites can be expensive; the cost is in many dollars per a gram to purchase, if you can find them.

Meteorite in its natural state does not work well for blades. This metal usually shatters when hit with a hammer, even at high heat, so it still needs to be refined. It is safer to use the can weld method to start. This prevents you from shattering the hot metal, and scattering it all over the floor of the shop while working with it.

When buying meteorite, check its composition. You want a solid block of iron (to the eye) instead of a rocky iron ore type. Using a magnet for a fast check can help, but a lab analysis is a reasonable request with the prices the sellers are asking. This is not a production run type of metal.

Start by breaking up the space rock into small pieces. Cut up some wrought iron rod and collect in a newspaper the band saw powders. While you can purchase steel powders from many on-line supply shops, using the wrought iron made more sense due to its silicon content. When I had worked with the meteorite, I had previously tested the wrought iron to see if it would harden, so I knew it had a usable carbon content, which was important for making the meteorite into a usable blade steel.

Welding closed the end of a 1.5 inch square pipe, and spray the nonstick coating on the inside. Add the mixed pieces of meteorite and the wrought iron powders in the 1.5" square pipe and pack in place to

Illustration 82: Pipe cut.

remove voids. Add a few drops of WD-40® to use up any oxygen. Weld the opposite end and drill a 1/16" hole on both ends for gas release, this is the same as the basic can weld.

Combining one part of meteorites with three parts old wrought iron reduces the effects of the trace elements and brings back the nickel content to a more manageable amount. The combination also adds silicon from the wrought iron into the mix.

Put the can into the fire. Your coal forge should be running hot with nice clean coke or charcoal. Bring the can up to welding temperature slow and easy, tap gently while turning the can a quarter turn after each tap, to heat evenly and firm up the contents while not breaking the outside of the can. As you proceed the heat travels through this can easier because you are also reducing the voids.

Illustration 83: Ready to weld closed.

Watch the gases escape with a little flame. After a while your forging will produce a solid mass drawn out and ready to fold. After only 7 or 8 folds this should become a reasonably homogeneous bar that you can use like high nickel steel bar. This is similar to the way wrought iron blooms were worked down from the spongy mass into usable iron.

After a pattern welded blade gets beyond 600 layers the pattern tends to "wash out," meaning it is hard to see the defined layers when they get so fine because our eyes only see so much detail. It is like looking at a tree from far away.

We see the green tops but not any leaves. As we move closer we may see leaves and bark, but from a distance, because there is to much detail to process, we only see trunk and tree.

The meteorite layers resulting from the can welding and folding appear the same way. With a magnifying glass you should see layers but not with the naked eye. Because it is too fine to notice this layering of the meteorite, the piece should appear to be a almost a mono steel layer. The only true way to get a homogeneous bar with that rock is to melt it with the wrought iron in a crucible.

For a finished blade you can now treat the meteorite bar as a single layer of steel. For example, if you used it to make a 100 layer blade, you would have 50 layers of a high carbon steel such as 1095, and 50 layers of this blended meteorite in the finished blade.

Remember the meteorite was first worked to at least 600 layers. Because it is hard to see the 600 layers in the bar you started with, and those layers are now 100 times thinner, effectively the bar appears as one solid layer to the eye. This method is a perfect alternative to building or hiring a foundry to melt a meteorite into usable bars for us.

Now cut, stack and weld again to bring this bar to 300 layers before forging it into a shape ready to pattern for a knife. This will be getting a shark tooth edge, for lack of a better word.

This technique is a variation on cutting a ladder pattern. Make the cuts to almost half the depth, coming up the blade side to a bit over half the width of the face, getting shallower as you reach the middle of the bar. This will give a saw tooth look to the pattern. I do not like to rely on random chance to give my blades a nice pattern, so I force it by using the following technique.

Illustration 84: Patterning.

After flattening, draw the billet out to about 1/4 inch thickness, then proceed to the final shaping. In picture 84, you can see how the saw tooth effect follows the angles of the cutting edge of the knife. By planning on variations of the direction of the cuts, you would be able to produce a very pleasing and natural appearing pattern in the blade shown in photo 85.

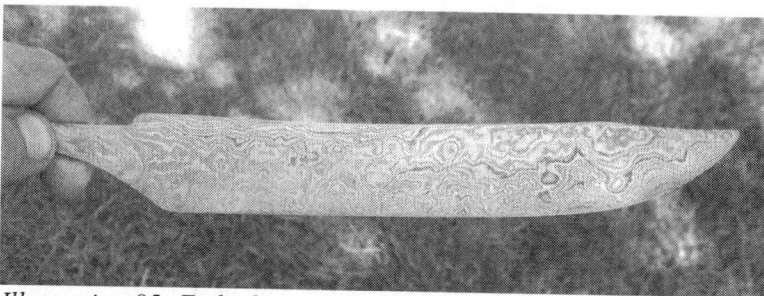

Illustration 85: Etched meteorite blade ready for mounting.

Proof of Meteoric Content

You may be asked to establish the provenance for the origin of the nickel in the blade. Since meteoric origins are highly unique, the blade should command a premium price just to offset the cost of raw materials. The skillful incorporation of celestial materials should add even more, but how do we prove it is of celestial origins to get that price?

There are multiple problems proving there are any celestial materials in the blade including:

Trust your Sources

When I got this meteorite from my supplier, I was told it is *Campo del Ceilo* from Argentina (one of the largest falls in the world). I have an analysis of those, but still have to have faith in the supplier to provide me with that material.

Be true to your word. Your word is all you have. Even if you filmed the process, you cannot prove someone did not edit it and use that billet elsewhere.

Quality of Craftsmanship

You made the blade. Is that blade really any good, or is your work junk. Just because you used expensive materials does not guarantee a high price for your blade. You have to be honest with yourself about what your result is against a world market. You still must make a quality blade. No matter if it is a meteorite damascus, if it is not usable as a blade or has poor fit and finish, it is just a piece of expensive metal.

Proof

If a person really wants to try to check the contents, they can cut a section from the blade (most likely ruining it as a blade) and test it. Now that person has the cost of your blade plus the cost of testing. They will get a measurement of the mix of wrought iron you used to work out the meteorite, and the carbon steel it was layered with to make the knife billet.

When they get a read out of elements in the sample, it would tell them this sample contains X% of iron, carbon, manganese (expected from the 1095), silicon (expected from the wrought iron), nickel, cobalt, iridium, and gallium.

These amounts are in relative proportion to a known ratio of those rarer elements found in meteorites but could also have been added from other sources, because there is nothing exclusive from the Campo meteorite fall. These elements are also found in other sources on Earth. Even if you could run some test to prove all these things, all the you have has to sell a blades is, in the end, your reputation.

It was the idea of "can I do this" that was my motivation behind making this meteorite into a blade.

Blade Harmonics

Making large blades is not the same as making small ones. As the blade gets longer there are harmonic nodes that come into play. You cannot just make a blade large without planning for the vibrations you will get from them. For the most part it is not a real problem if you are aware of them and pay attention, but if you just cut an edge on a flat bar of steel (like many first time smiths do when making a first knife) you are going to have a big problem.

Parallel sided steel bars of long lengths get vibrations. The easiest way to reduce vibrations is to break up the parallel sides with use of the distal taper we already covered in Chapter 7. Keep the maximum vibration point away from the hand and make it the null zone of vibrations instead. I can explain what is happening in the steel with mathematics but, in simple terms, this is the tuning fork effect. You all probably have hit a baseball with a bat and had your hand "buzz"; it is not pleasant and is indicative of a harmonic node.

This is one of the aspects that are in play when I say that sword making is not the same as knife making. Weight is another issue as useful, working swords were, and should be, quite light.

Making use of tapering along almost all dimensions and planning your structural design with fullers, aids in reducing vibrations.

Paying attention to the distal taper is the start of how to relocate and perhaps remove them. The wide tapers affect this as well, and is one more reason why some designs people create for video games do not work well in real life for swords, knives and anything in between.

Blades have been used by mankind for thousands of years. What works has been repeated for manufacture. What did not work well has been dropped. If you have parallel edges and sides there will be more vibrations than if it is all tapered smoothly. Some subtle bevel adjustments can affect them also. This is just a start of what to look for when making a sword.

Harmonics do play a big part in proper sword making. If you make the grip on a node, then the sword will stay in your hand even when struck or striking a hard object. If you make it a peak, then the sword will want to leave your hand during use; this is not a good thing.

After you get the blade close to how you wish it to look (remembering to remove about .030 inch off all sides to remove the decarb layer after heat treat) bonk (that is a technical term) the new blade against a block of wood and try to feel vibrations.

One third of the way from the guard toward the tip seems to be a sweet spot for causing this so try to impact it there to see how bad the blade vibrates. If the vibration is pronounced, then thin that area more. If not check a few other areas. If it is not very noticeable, then just make a few more passes with the grinder/belt sanding machine to clean up the blade. Only a few minutes effort can tune an OK blade and make it a great feeling blade.

Fullers

Fullers are a grooved depression in the blade. Most run from the guard to the tip, while others may only go part way down the blade.

There are many misconceptions existing about fullers. Some people erroneously call this indentation in the blade a blood groove,

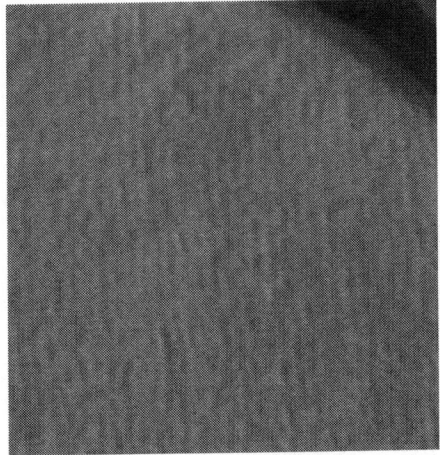

Illustration 86: Half inch wide fullers.

possibly from thinking it allowed blood to escape a wound faster, or prevent a vacuum from forming that could hold the blade in the wound. I hate this term for a fuller almost as much as I hate polishing blades that have them. Flesh does not seal up to the blade edge of the blade to create a vacuum. Nor will a fuller allow faster bleeding. Others assume the fuller will assist to open a wound to allow increased damage, which is

more nonsense. The fuller is used to make a blade lighter, and to stiffen the blade, much like a modern 'I beam'.

To put a fuller into a blade, hammer the recess into the side of the blade using

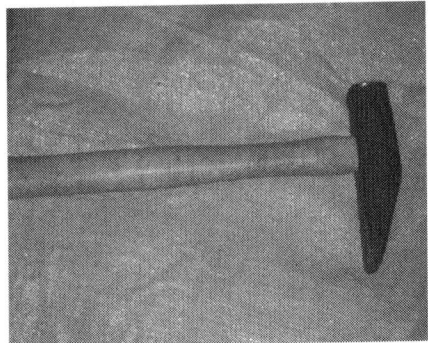

Illustration 87: Fullering tool.

fullering tools. As the depression is hammered into place, the blade widens as the metal from the fuller itself is displaced. The tool looks somewhat like a hammer with a rounded peen on the end, but it is not a hammer, the face is not one with which to hit, but to be struck. There are anvil mounted swages for fullering both sides simultaneously, as shown in picture 88.

After hammering in the basic groove for a guide, finish up with a contact wheel, as with a Viking broad sword. It is much easier to get the fullers ground and polished before starting work on the face and bevels of the blade. This way allows a safety net of squaring up the edges after you finish the polish. This is easier than if you did the entire blade at once, but try it if you wish.

Illustration 88: Dual sided spring fuller for anvil hardy.

Adding fullers to a blade can enhance their beauty and value, as well as adding another dimension to your craft.

Heat Treating Big Blades

When heat treating larger blades, you may find that many times the blades are longer than the forges sweet spot of glowing coals. You can fully heat up to 18 inch blades in an average coal forge before you need a larger forge. The blade does not have to sit in just one position. After getting a section close to hardening temperature, move it over about 6 inches and heat the next section, then move it again. After reaching the end, the first part is still over 900°F. Now it is time to slowly move the blade back and forth through the sweet spot. Soon the 18 inch blade is at an even heat of about 1550°F over its entire length and can then be quenched. Larger items will require a larger forge. Or you can dig a trench long enough to heat the blade in its entirety.

Machinery

Belt Grinder

Lot of folks build their own belt grinders. Keep in mind that we are knife makers and want a grinder mainly for that, different uses may alter the build. Standard knife machines use 2 x72 inch belts, and they are available in the widest variety of grits and weights for knife makers. If you use cheap belts you will not get good grinds.

For knife grinding you will need several things that are really not options if you want one that is worth building.

If you wish to hollow grind knives, you need a cushioned faced contact wheel the correct size for the thickness and width of the blades you will grind. A metal faced wheel will not work for this. The resistance of the coating on contact wheels is measured in durometers. Too soft or too hard will not work well. My wheels are 70 durometers in diameters of 5/8 inch diameter for finger holes up through a 10 inch contact wheel, and quite a few sizes in between. You can contact some of the well-known knife grinder makers and see what they specify for durometer ratings for their wheels. Then when you find a wheel you need to see how it stacks up to what we know works.

For idler wheels you can use steel or aluminum. Remember one of them needs to be crowned so the belts will track well. If you are going to flat grind you need a platen the width of the belt and sufficient length to work. Look at pictures of commercial grinders for an eyeball guess on length. The platen needs to be thick enough not to bend and warp with the pressure and heat of grinding. If I was to build a grinder now I would use half inch thick steel plate and high enough carbon to heat treat.

The tracking mechanism has to be spot on. If the wheels are out of line the grinder will give you problems. Tracking is a fine adjustment to move belt from side to side or take care of an inconsistency in a belt. All wheels must have good quality bearings to run on and properly fit to the axles. The drive wheel must be firmly fixed to the drive shaft. The frame of the machine needs to be very solid. Grinders work hard, which puts a lot of stress on the frame.

Some steels or belts, and even some handle materials will require different belt speeds. To work well with all of that a grinder needs to be changed easily for belt speeds. That can be with different pulleys that let you move belts easily, or with variable speed motors. I had bogged down the 1Hp motor on the old machine so often I purchased a 1.5Hp motor with the machine I now use. A 2 HP with speed adjustments would have been nicer. And let us not leave out a solid stand on which to hold all of this fine machinery.

You may figure out that a cheap grinder is not worth the time it takes unless you keep a lot of things in mind. And if you took half a year to build one that is even passable for knife work, that was time you could have been making blades. I feel you would be better off to work a part time job and buy something that you can begin to learn on the day you get it.

Drill Press

A drill press will drill tang holes safely and straight. Using hand held drills makes it very hard to keep holes aligned. Also, it is good to purchase a machinist's vise to mount on the press table to hold the work.

Remember steel needs slow speeds, so make sure the press you get can go slow enough; 300 rpm is not too slow. I do not use liquids for cooling.

Buffer

This is the most dangerous tool in the shop. This machine is designed to grab whatever you were holding and throw it into your gut at high velocity. But since it also does a very nice job of polishing the final product, I use it anyway. Remember to keep the work low when buffing, below the mid point of the wheel, to allow the thrown blade to go into the floor rather than into you.

Use only light pressure - do not use a heavy hand with this one. There are many types of buffs, including sisal, muslin and wool. Which to use depends on the compound needed, so experiment and decide which is best. In most cases the sewn wheels are more aggressive than the loose cloth buffs.

Quench Tank

The quench tank needs to be fire proof and have a tight fitting lid to extinguish flare ups and flash fires. It should be of a large enough volume to quench a few blades without overheating. Also ensure the base is solid so it cannot tip over. There is little in this world worse than having gallons of flaming oil pouring across the floor of the shop.

My long quench tank was made from a section of 6 inch diameter steel pipe, cut 40 inches high. After welding an over sized steel plate to close the bottom, it is very stable, and deep enough to quench swords, it holds almost 3 gallons of oil.

First Aid

No matter how careful we smiths are, when we work with fire and knives, sooner or later we will get hurt. Keeping a simple First Aid kit handy is a good idea. A First Aid kit could contain the following:

- Bandages
- Medical tape

- Small scissors
- Wooden finger splints
- Sterile gloves
- Sterile water
- Hydrogen peroxide
- Tweezers
- Cold pack
- Alcohol wipes
- Antiseptic cream

I have a few other unrelated Certifications in addition to being a bladesmith; I am an American Red Cross Instructor as well as a former Medic licensed by the state of Indiana. I am not a Doctor, nor do I pretend to have all the answers. I suggest everyone be prepared for accidents by taking a First Aid and CPR class. I will present an overview of a few things about which you may wish to know, for informational purposes.

Cuts & Abrasions

For a minor cut or an abrasion from a belt grinder for example, first you must clean the wound to remove contaminants. Then bandage the area until it can heal.

Bleeding should cease after 5 minutes. If bleeding does not stop after a few minutes of light pressure elevate and continue pressure. If the cut is deep or bleeding does not stop get professional help. Stitches may be needed to close the wound.

As I stated earlier, a buffer is the most dangerous machine I have. If it grabs and throws a blade, it can kill. If somehow you have a body part, such as a finger, removed, collect the amputated part with a clean cloth, and bring it to the hospital; it may be possible to reattach it.

If the accident results in a puncture, leave the item in place, as it is likely acting as a plug. Removal of the item may result in faster loss of bodily fluids and even death, so leave it stuck where it is and call the ambulance ... fast!

Burns

There are three basic types of burn you can get: first degree, second degree, and third degree. Here is a brief overview of each type of burn

First degree burns: These burns cause redness, with no serious tissue damage, and must be kept clean. If the burn is full circumference treat it as a second degree burn.

Full circumference is a condition where the damaged area has encircled a limb or other section of the body, and like girdling a tree, can cause much more long term problems than is apparent from the injury itself.

Second degree burns: These burns cause blistering, discoloration, swelling, and seepage – and need medical treatment to avoid secondary infections.

Outpatient care to overnight, or longer, hospital stay is possible. Watch for shock. If this results in a full circumference treat it as a as third degree burn, the damaged areas can contract, cutting off blood flow to the wound.

Third degree burns: These burns cause deep tissue destruction, are obviously burned, and normally result in permanent damage; even loss of the affected body part is possible. With this type of burn, you most likely will need long term hospitalization.

In addition to these, the percentage of body damaged and the types of burns can combine to place an injured party in other risk categories.

Since a burn can result in life threatening long term problems not always apparent at the time of the injury, follow these steps:

- Remove the heat source from the body.
- Clean the injury using cool (not iced) water. Set, or better yet, lay the injured person down with his or her legs elevated. You do not want to add falling to the injury list.
- Inspect the injury. If only red marks are present, you may wish to deal with it yourself, as that is the sign of a first degree burn. But if you see any blistering (second degree burn) or worse injury, then cover lightly with a protective clean cloth and get it seen by a professional as soon as possible.

Before deciding on aloe or any so called burn creams, I need to inform you that if you have to go get professional help, the first thing that will happen to you is the scrubbing off of the butter, aloe, creams, etc. that some well-meaning but misinformed person put on the burn. They need to clean the wound from that additional contamination. Your skin is the largest organ of the human body, and one of its functions is to protect the body from outside contamination. Because of the burn, the skin is now unable to do its job of protecting your body.

You must get the area as clean as you can. Surgical removal of the now dead/dying material (meaning your skin/muscle etc. that was burned) will be necessary by the attending Physician when you get to the hospital. Anything you put on a burn site, may have to be removed later, because anything worse than a simple first degree burn has unseen damage inside the body that must be addressed before serious infection occurs.

Eye Contamination

You may end up with smoke or dust in your eyes. Flushing with sterile water to remove the item usually is enough to help. A corneal scratch may hurt long after the foreign object is removed. Some things may need professional removal. It is best to see a doctor if you still feel something in the eye after flushing. If you have any questions call the hospital and talk to the professionals. If you need to go to the hospital, cover both eyes as the injured eye will track along with the good eye, which may cause additional injury.

Air Quality

We smiths should all have good ventilation in the shop, as well as a sensor for carbon monoxide/carbon dioxide buildup in our shop and a smoke detector. We may even get a face of smoke from the fire. If this happens or the alarm goes off, or you feel light headed, turn off the air/fuel leave the shop, sit down and rest somewhere and get yourself some fresh air. You can make sure the fire is out after you get some clean air, if you worry about the fire first you may not get out of the shop in time. This is another good reason to have a fire proof area around the fire pot.

Heat Exhaustion

Heat exhaustion, dehydration, and heat stroke can hit very fast on even a mild day working at the forge. While we are working, we all need to drink plenty of water. If you get light headed or notice you have stopped sweating, get out of the smithy, sit down, and take a break. This could be early signs of a heat emergency. Later signs can include dizziness, disorientation, and loss of consciousness; by then, you may not be able to do anything to help yourself.

Animal Bites/Stings

More than once I have seen spiders in my shop. While most are harmless, a few can be deadly. Black Widow, Brown Recluse, and the Hobo Spider can kill when you place your hand in that glove they were hidden in. A snake or a raccoon could be in the shop, in addition to other animals that can take refuge in our shops, and most will not react well when surprised and we make them feel cornered. Most of the time, they want to stay away from you and will not harm you, but if you are bitten, ice the area to reduce swelling, try to identify the animal, and call your doctor. Do not cut the wound and try to suck out the poison, that is an old wives tale, and will cause more harm than good.

Think about where you plan to store your first aid kit in the shop. If you are injured and fall to the ground, will you be able to reach the kit? Phone placement is another planning consideration; when you need to summon aid, it is too late to find out your phone is also out of reach.

Liability

I need to address liability issues of our work. Making blades is fun. Getting paid for making them is even better. After the sale though, you are not done. As knife makers we may have legal liability in some situations. If that blade breaks and the user gets hurt we could be sued and held liable for damages. It is not "just make it and take the money." We must make sure our blades will hold up to the intended use. Put a disclaimer clause in the contract and bill of sale, that may reduce a negligence claim.

Ask the client:

- What the blades purpose will be.
- Why the clients wants this particular blade.
- What do they expect from this blade.

This helps us make changes on the design specifications that will make our client, and our insurance companies happier. I know from experience that insurance is not cheap, nor easy to find for blade smiths. Insurance may be the only thing that allows us to keep our homes if a claim is filed, even if the injury was beyond our control, although an attorney explained to me that it is very hard to prove causation in a negligence case.

A person selling a blade to military personnel is placing that person's life in their hands with the blade.

While hand-to-hand sword combat is no longer common place, getting a cut in a military situation is not a simple case of grabbing a bandage and triple antibiotic ointment. Having a cut can affect a person's ability to use that injured body part, which can have a detrimental effect in a combat situation.

It is important to make sure the blade being ordered is legal to make. For example, a number of years ago a client who had the money, wanted a sword cane. After questioning the client I had to pass, because it is illegal to publicly carry a blade that large where he lived. The sword being hidden inside the cane added concealed carry problems as well.

Each country and state has different laws, and some cities may have more in addition to the general state and national regulations. I want to make you aware that there is more than just getting money for the blades when making knives. You can be held accountable for what you make and sell.

As a maker you need to ask *"Am I ready to make that blade the way it should be made?"* Do not take on a commission and then later hope to get it done on time. Making sure you can do it right before taking on the job is also part of responsible trade-craft.

We have generations of smiths who have gone before us, that have taken the time to pass down to us what they learned. Let us not shame them or ourselves by producing anything but the finest blades we can make.

In Closing

I hope that I have been able to give you something to take with you to your shop in order to make better blades.

Maybe I was able to show you a safer way of performing an operation. Perhaps I explained a technique you had always wondered about but had not tried.

While it was not possible to include everything I know in this book, I have attempted to share the basics of what has worked for me, in the hope others will grow from this.

Thank you for reading. Please stop by my web site and have a look around at www.fenrisforge.com Feel free to post an Email with any comments or questions.

Steve

Appendix

Blade Steels

Analysis taken from a mean average of reports from suppliers I have used.

1095
C .99 Mn .42 Si.22

1084FG
C .87 Mn 80 Si .27 Cr .15

1075
C .76 Mn .35 Si .24

5160
C .60 Mn .80 Si .20 Cr .80

52100
C 0.95 Mn .34 Si .07 Cr 1.42

80CVR2
C .80 Si .32 Mn .54 V .15

8670M
C .70Mn .5 Si .25 Ni .85 Mo .05

15N20
C .75 Mn .75 Si .25 Ni 1.5

L-6 (from Crucible* they only sell in round bars)
C .75 Mn .65 Si .25 Cr .80 Ni 1.75 Mo .30 V .25

L-6 (from other sources)
C .70 Mn .50 Si .Cr .50 Ni 2.00

O-1
C .90 Mn 1.25 Si .30 Cr .50 Va .20 W .50

A-2
C 1.0 Mn .85 Si .35 Cr 5.25 Va .25 W 6.4 Mo 1.10

D-2
C 1.50 Mn .40 Si .40 Cr 12.00 Va .95 Mo .90

M-2
C .85 Mn .30 Si .30 Cr 4.15 Va 1.95 W 6.4 Mo 5.0

W-2
C 0.91 Mn .2 Si 0.29

A203E
C .09 Mn .64 Si .34 Ni 3.58 Cr .030 Mo .010

201 Nickel
Ni 99.50

440C
C 1.0 Mn .50 Si .30 Cr 17.50 Mo .50

Wrought Iron
Si 2.0   C varies

Steel Standards.

This is only for cross reference of comparisons for understanding. It not an exact exchange.

USA SAE/ANSI	Sweden SS	Great Briton BS/EN	Germany DIN
1060	1678	EN43D	Ck60
1095	1870	060 A96	Ck101
5160	- - -	EN48	55Cr3
52100	2258	EN31	100Cr6
6150	2230	EN47	50CrV4
A-2	2260	BA2	X100CrMoV5.1
L-6	2550	- - -	55NiCrMoV6
M-2	2722	BM2	S6/5/2/5
W-1	1880	BW1A	C 105 W1

Glossary of terms

A

Austempering A heat-treating process where the steel is cooled from austenitic fast enough to avoid the formation of pearlite, but held above the martensetic transformation point for long periods

Austenite The non-magnetic state steel takes when the carbon is in a face-centered cubic form. Some stainless steels are naturally this state, while other steels are heated to get to this state. Also the first phase formed as liquid steel turns solid.

B

Bainite A very tough form of steel that forms during the austempering process and can be created by holding the quenching temperature at 600°F to 800°F, resulting in upper bainite. If the temperature is held at 450°F-600°F, this will allow the formation of lower bainite.

Bevel The angled side of a blade leading into the cutting edge.

Bolster This decorative placement does little if anything to protect the hand form the blade. Mostly decorative.

Brass An alloy of varying amounts of copper and zinc. Yellow brass is 67% copper and 33% zinc, and the Red brass is 85% copper and 15% zinc. There are other alloys available.

Bronze An alloy of varying amounts of copper and tin. The copper content ranges from 70% to 97% with the balance being tin. There are variations such as Phosphor bronze and Aluminum bronze.

C

Carbon (C) Element number 6. Its addition into iron creates steel. Carbon increases hardenability and strength. For blades to harden they need to contain about 0.4% or more of carbon.

Carbon Migration The term for the diffusion of a higher carbon rich environment to a lower carbon area. High temperatures cause acceleration of this effect. Must be watched for when at pattern welding temperatures.

Case Hardening The process of leaving iron, or mild steel in a carbon rich environment at high temperatures for prolonged periods, to encourage carbon migration into the metal. In times past, this was one of the few ways to create steel.

Cast Iron A form of iron-based metal generally containing above 2.5% carbon.

Cementite Fe3C Also known as "iron carbide," this presents itself in two forms, plate and lathe. These are hard and brittle carbides. In hypereutectoid steels there will be pearlite and some cementite when slow cooling of the steel from austenite.

Chape This protects the tip of a scabbard.

Choil The angle in a blade at the junction of the wedge-shaped cutting part with the tang or the corresponding part of any knife

Chromium/Chrome (Cr) Element number 24. Its addition to steel adds in deep hardening. In amounts exceeding 13%, it creates stainless steel.

Cobalt (Co) Element number 27. Its addition makes steel very hard, wear-resistant, and high-strength alloys.

Curie Temperature The critical temperature at which steel loses its magnetic properties.

D

Dagger A bladed weapon generally under 18 inches long. Most are double edged.
Dirk Another term for a dagger.
Distal Taper A blade's gradual narrowing with distance from its base toward the tip. Generally referring to thickness.
Durometer This is a measurement of hardness for synthetic wheels.

E

Eutectic point The proportion of constituents in an alloy or other mixture that yields the lowest possible complete melting point. In all other proportions, the mixture will not have a uniform melting point; some of the mixture will remain solid while some remains liquid. At the eutectic point, the solidus and liquidus temperatures are the same (normally 0.83% carbon for steel). See chart.

F

Ferrite Iron An iron form containing 0.02% dissolved carbon

G

Gallium (Ga) Element number 31. A rare element found in Meteorites, and in trace amounts in bauxite and zinc ores.

German Silver Also known as "nickel silver." Various alloys are common. One alloy consists of 65% copper, 18% nickel and 17% zinc, another consists of 55% copper, 25%, zinc and 20% nickel.

H

Hardness The ability of a material to resist plastic deformation. The common measurement system used for measuring blades is the Rockwell "C" scale.
HSS Not really a grade, but a general term meaning high speed steel, often ANSI M2.
Hypereutectoid Steel with more than 0.83% carbon.

I

Iridium (Ir) Element number 77. It is commonly found only in meteorites. Iridium is used in high-strength alloys that can withstand high temperatures, and is notable for being the most corrosion-resistant element known. It is used in high temperature apparatus, electrical contacts, and as a hardening agent for platinum.
Iron (Fe) Element number 26,. The main component of Steel.

K

Knife A bladed weapon commonly found with a single cutting edge.

L

Locket Protective entrance to a scabbard
Low Alloy Steel Steel containing less than 2% alloying elements

M

Magnesium (Mg) Element number 12. Once produced from magnesium salts, this alkaline earth metal is used as an alloying agent to make aluminum-magnesium alloys. Used as an igniter in thermite welding. The free element is not found in nature.

Manganese (Mn) Element number 25. Added to steel as a deoxidizer and assists in hardening. Counters brittleness from sulfur.

Martensite The hardest form and strongest of the micro structures. Formed from austenite during quenching portion of heat treating steel.

Meteorite A piece of rock from outer space, usually from an exploded star or planet, that comes to earth as an asteroid or comet. The metallic types most commonly used in smithing contain about 93% iron, 6.3% nickel, and the remaining a balance of iridium, cobalt, and gallium, and along with a few other things. Occasionally used as layers in pattern welding.

Molybdenum (Mo) Element number 42. Deepens hardening, enhances corrosion resistance and increases wear resistance. It has the sixth highest melting point of any element, and is often used in high-strength steel alloys.

N

Nickel (Ni) Element number 28. Contributes to the silvery part of the pattern welded layers. Aids in strength and toughness when alloyed to steel

Nickel Silver See German Silver.

Normalizing Process of relaxing the stress created in metal during forging and grinding.

P

Pearlite Structure Alternating bands of ferrite and cementite, referred to as a pearlite structure, that form when simple steels are cooled slowly. Under a microscope this structure has a mother of pearl appearance, giving it its name.

Periodic Table The chart consisting of all the known elements laid out according to Family and various properties. Elements are listed by name and have a number assigned by atomic weight.

Phase A physical condition of the atomic arrangement in a crystal.

Phase Diagram An iron-carbon phase diagram for carbon steel which shows the condition under which the phases are stable.

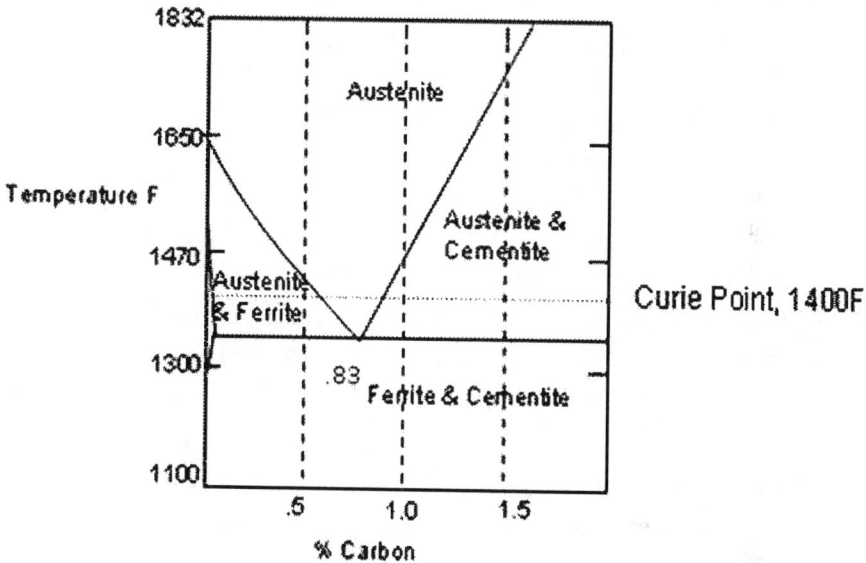

Q

Quench Term used for the controlled rapid cooling of metals.

R

Ricasso An unsharpened length of blade just above the guard or handle on a knife, dagger, sword, or bayonet.

S

Silicon (Si) Element number 14. It deoxidizes and improves hardness. High levels of silicon are added to steels for increased electrical conductivity.

Stake anvil A stand alone forming tool, may even be available as a hardy tool

Stainless Steel The term used for steel alloys with available chrome above 10.5%. It is very difficult and costly to heat treat stainless steel, therefore inexpensive blades that have been made from stainless steel were not likely heat treated properly. The end result has given stainless steels an undeserved bad reputation for blades.

Steel Created when carbon is added to iron.

Sulfur (S) Element number 16. It can make knife steels brittle. Considered a contaminant.

Swage Blacksmiths forming tool, often custon made.

Sword A blade usually over 18 inches long.

T

Tin (Sn) Element number 50. Commonly combined with copper to make bronze.

Titanium (Ti) Element number 22. Titanium weighs about half that of iron but is almost as strong. While rarely used for blades, titanium is often used for decoration. It forms carbides and reduces hardness in stainless steels. Titanium can be alloyed with other elements such as iron, aluminum, vanadium, molybdenum and others to produce strong lightweight alloys.

Tempering The gentle heating of a hardened blade to cause the stress from hardening to relax brittleness, increase toughness, and relieve stress.

Troosite Archaic term referring to tempered martensite.

Tungsten (W) Element number 74. Also known as Wolfram. This metal increases wear resistance, hot strength and hot hardness of steel. It has the highest melting point of all the non-alloyed metals and the second highest of all the elements after carbon.

V

Vanadium (V) Element number 23. When added to steel this metal increases hardenability, and fine grain structure.

W

Wootz A high carbon crucible steel created in a process assumed to originate in India. The results can be recreated today in a process involved sealing iron and carbon in a chamber and heating to extremely high temperatures. The excessive carbides in the material produced and their segregation produce a visible pattern in the steel, resembling a fine layered pattern welding. These blades also produce a very abrasion-resistant edge.

Wolfram (W) See Tungsten

Z

Zinc (Zn) Element number 30. Zinc fumes are released when heating a zinc-plated item and are highly toxic. When alloyed with other metals, it is safe at normal room temperatures.

References

The Pattern Welded Blade,
Dr Jim P. Hrisoulas (1997)

The Master Blade smith,
Dr Jim P. Hrisoulas (1994)

The Complete Bladesmith,
Dr Jim P. Hrisoulas (1991)

Metallurgy of Steel for Bladesmiths & Others who
Heat Treat and Forge Steel,
Prof. John D. Verhoeven

Metals Handbook, Vol. 1, 10th Edition, Properties and
Selection: Irons, Steels, and High Performance Alloys,
p.141, Classification and Designation of
Carbon and Low Alloy Steels, ASM
International, (1990).

Jacquet-Lucas Award: Metallography of a Modern
Pattern-Welded Steel Knife Blade,
Thomas Nizolek
Advanced Materials & Processes,
Volume 167, Issue 2, February 2009
www.asminternational.org
Thanks to Sue Sellers of ASM International for
her efforts in locating this report.

Carbon Diffusion Between the Layers in Modern
Pattern-Welded Damascus Blades
Materials Characterization,
John D Verhoeven & Howard Clark
Volume 41, Issue 5, November 1998, pg 183-191)

The Alloying Elements in Steel,
by Edgar C. Bain, 1939

Metallurgy Theory and Practice,
by Dell K. Allen, June 1969

Suggested reading

'The Backyard Blacksmith"
by Lorelei Sims. August 1, 2009

"The Skills of a Blacksmith, vol 1"
by Mark Aspery. March 24, 2007

"The Skills of a Blacksmith, vol 2"
by Mark Aspery. May 30, 2009

"The Skills of a Blacksmith, vol 3"
by Mark Aspery. 2013

"The Fifty dollar knife shop"
by Wayne Goddard. Jan 1, 2001

Word Index

G
Gas 56,57,132,139,159,167
German Silver (see nickel silver)
Grain 28,33,40,57,59,61,65,66,68,70-72,81,105,107
    125,134,147
Grit 45,48-50,57,70,75-79,84,85,91,92,100,101,104,
    105,108,110,122,123,126,128,132,163,176
Guard 22,87-97,99-101,105-107,110,111,112,113,122,
    145,173,174

H
Hamon 27,30,67,149
Hardening 27,30,31,36,46,56-61,64,66,69,71,73,135
        151,175
Hardness 57,69,81
Harmonics 172,173
Heat treat 10,11,16,25,27,33,37,43,44,46,47,50,53,58,59,
        63-66,69-73,76,78,80,82,88-90,94,104,107
        109,150,151,173,175,177
Hidden pins 111
Hidden tang 105
Horn 102,103,105-109
Hydrochloric acid 130,163

I
Insurance 185
Iridium 165,171
Iron 26,58-60,68,94,111,112,129-131,142,144,154,159
    163,165-168,171

J
Jig 77,78,137

K
Kerosene 138,140,153,159

R
Rail road spikes 26,37
Ricasso 34,36,39,42,46,47,87,92,95,101,112
Rose-one 14

S
SAE 26,29,53
Salt tank 68
Sand 76,104,121,123,126,127,158
Scabbards 108,125,128
Scales 76,92,100,101,103,109-113,115-117
Sharpening 15,43,45,46
Sheaths 119,121,128
Silicon 28,29,166,167,171
Silicon Carbide 76
Slotted guard 94,95,99,113
Small wheel (contact) 47,101
Smithing group 19
Spacer 103,105-109,111,114,117,122
Stabilizing 102,103,125
Steel choice 62,162
Straightening 41,72,73
Stainless Steel 27,28,57,63-65,82,90,96,137,161,162
Straw ash 159
Steel codes 29,30
Subzero quench 62,64
Sulfur 27
Sword 26,92,93,111,112,125,126,128,145,172,173,
175,179,186

T
Tangs 49,69,99,105
Tempering 28,31,51,61,62,65,68,69,90
Testing 18,36,63,65,70-72,80-82,134,171
Thermal 58,61-64,66,147
Titanium 26
Tongs 8,13,18,32,36,39,42,65
Torch 68,69

Made in the USA
Lexington, KY
12 September 2018